Life of

WILLIAM PITT.

BY

Lord Macaulay.

Preceded by the Life of

The Earl of Chatham.

NEW YORK:
DELISSER AND PROCTER,
Succeſſors to Stanford & Swords,
508 Broadway.

EDITOR'S PREFACE.

This volume of the Household Library contains a Life of the elder Pitt, by a writer in the Encyclopedia Britannica, who signs himself J. B——e; and a Life of the younger Pitt, by Lord Macaulay. The former is brief, and is here used as a suitable introduction to the latter.

The Pitts cannot be ranked among heroes of any kind; yet their lives are peculiarly interesting, inasmuch as they are intimately connected with an important and eventful period of English history. "The situation of Pitt [Earl of Chatham] at the close of the reign of George the Second," says Macaulay, "was the most enviable ever occupied by any public man in England. He had conciliated the King; he domineered over the House of Commons; he was adored by the people; he was admired by all Europe. He was the first Englishman of his time; and he made England the first country in the world. The great Commoner—the name by which he was often designated—might look down with scorn on coronets and garters. The nation was drunk with joy and pride. . . ." "A few years sufficed to change the whole aspect of affairs. A nation convulsed by faction, a throne assailed by the fiercest invective, a House of Commons hated and despised by the nation, England set against Scotland, Britain set against America, a rival legislature sitting beyond the Atlantic, English blood shed by English bayonets, our armies capitulating, our conquests wrested from us, our enemies hastening to take vengeance for past humiliation, our flag scarcely able to maintain itself in our own seas—such was the spectacle Pitt lived to see."

The aspect of the world was changed during the long ministry of the younger Pitt. The name itself is associated with political revolutions. The fugitive Bourbons, the downfall of French aristocracy, Jacobin clubs, *guillotines*, floods of blood in the streets of Paris; the breaking up of the Germanic empire; the vanishing republic of Holland; the sundering of the old Helvetian League; the peremptory dissolution of the great Council of Venice; the founding of a new republic on the Western Continent, where ideas of political freedom—fugitives from the Old World to the New—seemed to find an asylum; fresh creations on both sides of the ocean,—here Washington, there Napoleon,—here democracy, there an empire—here States uniting in representative government, there a confederation of the Rhine; great parliamentary struggles, and splendid political victories and defeats; the gathering of armies and intrigues of courts; Franklin and Talleyrand; life-and-death conflicts between kings and peoples: all these things, and many more, are recalled at the bare mention of the Earl of Chatham and his more illustrious son.

We have given a sketch of Lord Macaulay's life, in another volume of the Household Library (Frederick the Great), and need not repeat it here. His Life of Pitt is a fresh production, written expressly for the Encyclopedia Britannica, and has been reprinted from an early copy. The article has already produced a sensation in England; many who are not subscribers to the Encyclopedia will doubtless be glad to obtain it in a convenient and attractive form.

O. W. WIGHT.

March, 1859.

PITT, EARL OF CHATHAM.

William Pitt, first Earl of Chatham, a celebrated British statesman and orator, was born on the 15th of November, 1708. He was the youngest son of Mr. Robert Pitt of Boconnock in Cornwall, the grandson of Mr. Thomas Pitt, governor of Fort St. George in the East Indies in the rein of Queen Anne, who sold an extraordinary diamond to the King of France for £135,-000, and thus obtained the name of *Diamond Pitt.* The subject of this notice was educated at Eton, whence, in January, 1726, he was removed to Trinity College, Oxford, which he entered as a gentleman commoner. Here the superiority of his mind soon attracted notice, and he was also remarked for his powers of elocution; but at the age of sixteen he experienced the first attacks of an hereditary and incurable gout, which continued at intervals to torment him during the remainder of his life. He quitted the university without taking a degree, and visited France and Italy, whence he returned without having received much benefit from his excursion. His father was now dead, and as he had left very little to the younger children, it became necessary that William should choose a profession. He decided for the army, and a cornet's commission was purchased for him in the Blues. But, small as his fortune was, his family had the power and the inclination to serve him At the general election of 1734, his elder brother Thomas was chosen both for Old Sarum and for Oakhampton. When parliament met in 1735, Thomas made his election for Oakhampton, and William was returned for Old Sarum. At the time when he obtained a seat in parliament he was not quite twenty-one years of age. The intention of bringing him thus early into parliament was to oppose Sir Robert Walpole, who had now been fourteen years at the head of affairs. In fact, his abilities soon attracted notice, and he spoke with great vehemence against the Spanish convention in 1738. It was on the occasion of the bill for registering seamen, in 1740, which he opposed as arbitrary and unjustifiable, that he is said to have made his celebrated reply to Walpole, who had taunted him on account of his youth; but the language of that reply, as it now stands, is not the diction of Pitt, who may have said something like what is ascribed to him, but of

Dr. Johnson, who then reported, or rather wrote, the debates for the *Gentleman's Magazine.* In 1746 Pitt was appointed joint vice-treasurer of Ireland; and in the same year treasurer and paymaster-general of the army, and a privy councillor. The office of paymaster he discharged with such inflexible integrity, even refusing many of the ordinary perquisites of office, that his bitterest enemies could lay nothing to his charge, and he soon became the darling of the people. The old Duchess of Marlborough, who carried to the grave the reputation of being decidedly the best hater of her time, and who most cordially detested Walpole and his associates, left Pitt a legacy of £10,000, in consideration of "the noble defence he had made for the support of the laws of England, and to prevent the ruin of his country." In the year 1755, Pitt, deeming it necessary to offer a strong opposition to the continental connections then formed by the ministry, resigned his places, and remained some time out of office. But his resignation having alarmed the people, he was, in December, 1756, called to fill a higher office, and ap pointed secretary of state. In this situation, however, he was more successful in obtaining the confidence of the public than in conciliating the favor of the King, some of whose predilections he had conceived himself bound to oppose. The consequence was, that soon afterwards Pitt was removed from office, whilst Legge, with some others of his friends, were at the same time dismissed. But the nation had a mind not to be deprived of his services. The most exalted notion had been formed of him throughout the country; his patriotism was believed to be as pure and disinterested as his abilities and eloquence were confessedly transcendent; and his colleagues shared in the same general favor. In a word, the opinion of the country was so strongly expressed, both directly and indirectly, that the King thought it prudent to yield; and on the 25th of June, 1757, Pitt was again appointed secretary of state, Legge became chancellor of the exchequer, and the other arrangements were made conformably to his wishes. Pitt was now in effect prime minister; and the change which soon took place in the aspect of public affairs evinced the ability of his measures, and the vigor of his administration. His spirit animated the whole nation, and his activity pervaded every department of the public service. His plans were ably conceived and promptly executed; and the depression which had been occasioned by want of energy in the cabinet, and ill success in the field, was followed by exertion, confidence, and triumph. The whole fortune of the war was changed. In every quarter of the globe success attended our arms. The boldest attempts were made, both by land and by sea, and almost every attempt proved fortunate. In America the French lost Quebec; in Africa they were deprived of their principal settlements; their power was abridged in the East Indies; in Europe their armies were defeated; and, to render their humiliation more complete, their navy, their commerce, and their finances were almost ruined. Amidst this full tide of success George II. died, on the 25th of October, 1760, and was succeeded by George III., who ascended the throne at a time when the French court had just succeeded in obtaining the co-operation of Spain.

The treaty commonly called "family compact" had been secretly concluded but the English minister, correctly informed of the hostile intentions of Spain, determined to anticipate that power, and strike a blow before this new enemy should be fully prepared for action. He therefore proposed in the council an immediate declaration of war against Spain, urging forcibly that the present was the favorable moment for humbling the whole House of Bourbon. But when he stated this opinion in the privy council, the other ministers, averse to so bold a measure, opposed the proposition of the premier, alleging the necessity of mature deliberation before declaring war against so powerful a state. Irritated by the unexpected opposition of his colleagues, Pitt replied, "I will not give them leave to think; this is the time; let us crush the whole House of Bourbon. But if the members of this board are of a different opinion, this is the last time I shall ever mix in its councils. I was called into the ministry by the voice of the people, and to them I hold myself answerable for my conduct. I am to thank the ministers of the late king for their support; I have served my country with success; but I will not be responsible for the conduct of the war any longer than while I have the direction of it." To this declaration the president of the council answered, "I find the gentleman is determined to leave us; nor can I say that I am sorry for it, since he would otherwise have certainly compelled us to leave him. But if he is resolved to assume the right of advising his Majesty, and directing the operations of the war, to what purpose are we called to this council? When he talks of being responsible to the people, he talks the language of the House of Commons, and forgets that at this board he is responsible only to the King. However, though he may possibly have convinced himself of his infallibility, still it remains that we should be equally convinced before we can resign our understandings to his direction, or join with him in the measure he proposes." The opposition he thus encountered the nation attributed to the growing influence of Lord Bute. But however this may have been, Pitt was a man of too high, not to say imperious a temper, to remain as the nominal head of a cabinet which he was no longer able to direct. Accordingly, on the 5th of October, 1761, he resigned all his appointments; and, as some reward for his services, his wife was created Baroness Chatham in her own right, whilst a pension of £3000 a year was settled on the lives of himself, his lady, and his eldest son.

No fallen minister, if fallen he could be called, ever carried with him more completely the confidence and regret of the nation, whose affairs he had so successfully administered. But at this time the King was also popular; and the war being continued by his new ministers with vigor and success, no discontent appeared until after the conclusion of the peace. The impulse given by Pitt had carried them forward in the same direction which he had pursued; but they were equally incapable of profiting by the advantages which had been already gained, or of prosecuting the war until the objects for which it was originally undertaken should be accomplished. The victories gained over France and Spain having greatly elated the nation, the feeling which almost universally prevailed amongst the people was, that we should either dictate peace as conquerors, or continue the war until our adversaries were more effectually humbled. This was likewise Pitt's opinion. Accordingly, when the preliminaries of peace came to be discussed in parliament, he went down to the House of Commons, though suffering severely from an attack of gout, and spoke for nearly three hours in the debate, giving his opinion on each article of the treaty in succession, and, upon the whole, maintaining that it was inadequate to the conquests of our arms, and the just expectations of the country. Peace was, however, concluded on the 10th of February, 1763, and Pitt continued unemployed.

After his resignation in 1761, Pitt conducted himself in a maner worthy of his high character. So far from giving a vexatious and undiscriminating opposition to the ministry which had succeeded his own, he maintained his popularity in dignified retirement, and came forward only when questions of great importance were to be discussed. One of these occurred in 1764, on the subject of general warrants, the illegality of which he denounced with all the energy and vigor of his eloquence. Another occasion, when he came forward in all his strength, was the consideration of the discontents which had arisen on account of the Stamp Act. In March 1766, the repeal of that act having been proposed by the Rockingham ministry, Pitt, though not connected with them, ably supported the measure, which was carried, but whether prudently or the contrary is still a matter of dispute. About this time Pitt had devised to him by will a considerable estate in Somersetshire, the property of Sir William Pynsent of Burton-Pynsent in that county, who, from admiration of his public character, disinherited his own relations, in order to bequeath to him the bulk of his fortune. After the dissolution of the

Rockingham ministry, a new administration was formed, and in 1766 Pitt was appointed lord privy seal. At the same time he was created a peer by the titles of Viscount Pitt of Burton-Pynsent, in the county of Somerset, and Earl of Chatham, in the county of Kent.

Whatever might be his motives in accepting a peerage, it is certain that it proved very prejudicial to his character, and that in consequence he sank as much in popularity as he rose in nominal dignity. The "great commoner," as he was sometimes called, had formed a rank for himself, on the basis of his talents and exertions, which titular honors might obscure, but could not illustrate; and, with the example of Pulteney before him, he should have been careful to preserve it untarnished by empty distinctions, shared by the mean and the worthless as well as by the great, the gifted, and the good. Lord Chatham, however, did not long continue in office after being elevated to the peerage. On the 2d of November, 1768, he resigned the place of lord privy seal, and never afterwards held any public employment; nor does he appear to have been at all desirous of returning to office. He was now sixty, and the gout, by which he had so long been afflicted, disabled him, by its frequent and violent attacks, for close and regular application to business. In the intervals of his disorder, however, he failed not to exert himself upon questions of great magnitude; and in 1775, 1776, and 1777, he most strenuously opposed the measures pursued by the ministers in the contest with America. His last appearance in the House of Lords was on the 2d of April, 1778. He was then very ill, and much debilitated; but the question was important, being a motion of the Duke of Richmond to address his Majesty to remove the ministers, and to make peace with America on any terms. His lordship made a long speech, in which he summoned up all his remaining strength to pour out his disapprobation of a measure so inglorious. But the effort overcame him, for in attempting to rise a second time, he fell down in a convulsive fit; and though he recovered for the time, his disorder continued to increase until the 11th of May, when he expired at his seat at Hayes. His death was lamented as a national loss. As soon as the news reached the House of Commons, which was then sitting, Colonel Barré made a motion, that an address should be presented to his Majesty, requesting that the Earl of Chatham should be buried at the public expense. But Mr. Rigby having proposed the erection of a statue to his memory, as more likely to perpetuate the sense of his great merits entertained by the public, this was unanimously agreed to. A bill was soon afterwards passed, by which £4000 a year was settled upon John, now Earl of Chatham, and the heirs of the late earl to whom that title might descend. His lordship was married in 1754 to Lady Hester, sister of Earl Temple, by whom he had three sons and two daughters.

The principal outlines of Pitt's character have been variously sketched, sometimes with, and sometimes without, any depth of shadow. The truth is, that there scarcely ever lived a person who had less claim to be painted altogether *en beau*, or who so little merited unsparing censure. Lord Macaulay says, "That he was a great man, cannot for a moment be doubted; but his was not a complete and well-proportioned greatness. The public life of Hampden or of Somers resembles a regular drama, which can be criticised as a whole, and every scene of which is to be viewed in connection with the main action. The public life of Pitt, on the other hand, is a rude though striking piece, abounding in incongruities, and without any unity of plan, but redeemed by some noble passages, the effect of which is increased by the tameness or extravagance of what precedes and of what follows. His opinions were unfixed; and his conduct, at some of the most important conjunctures of his life, was evidently determined by pride and resentment. He had one fault, which of all human faults is most rarely found in company with true greatness. He was extremely affected. He was an almost solitary instance of a man of real genius, and of a brave, lofty, and commanding spirit, without simplicity of character. He was an actor in the closet, an actor in the council, and an actor in parliament; and even in private society he could not lay aside his theatrical tones and attitudes. We know that one of the most distinguished of his partisans often complained that he could never obtain admittance to Lord Chatham's room till every thing was ready for the representation; till the light was thrown with Rembrandt-like effect on the head of the illustrious performer; till the flannels had been arranged with the air of Grecian drapery, and the crutch placed as gracefully as that of Belisarius or Lear." Yet, with all his faults and affectations, he possessed, in a very extraordinary degree, many of the elements of true greatness. He had splendid talents, strong passions, quick sensibility, and vehement enthusiasm for the grand and the beautiful. There was something about him which ennobled even tergiversation itself. He often went wrong, very far wrong; but, amidst the abasement of error, he still retained what he had received from nature, "an intense and glowing mind." In an age of low and despicable prostitution, the age of Dodington and Sandys, it was something to have a man who might perhaps, under some strong excitement, have been tempted to ruin his country, but who never would have stooped to pilfer from her; a man whose errors arose, not from a sordid desire of gain, but from a fierce thirst for power, glory, and vengeance. "History owes him this attestation, that, at a time when any thing short of direct embezzlement of the public money was considered as quite fair in public men, he showed the most scrupulous disinterestedness; that, at a time when it seemed to be generally taken for granted that government could be upheld only by the basest and most immoral arts, he appealed to the better and nobler parts of human nature; that he made a brave and splendid attempt to do, by means of public opinion, what no other statesman of his day thought it possible to do except by means of corruption; that he looked for support, not, like the Pelhams, to a strong aristocratical connection, not, like Bute, to the personal favor of the sovereign, but to the middle class of Englishmen; that he inspired that class with a firm confidence in his integrity and ability; that, backed by them, he forced an unwilling court and an unwilling oligarchy to admit him to an ample share of power; and that he used his power in such a manner as clearly proved that he had sought it, not for the sake of profit or patronage, but from a wish to establish for himself a great and durable reputation, by means of eminent services rendered to the state."

A great many unmeaning phrases have been employed, and much rhetorical exaggeration has been expended, in attempts to characterize Lord Chatham's style of eloquence. The following estimate by Lord Macaulay, from whom we have borrowed some of the foregoing observations, is at once deep, discriminating, and brilliant.

"In our time the audience of a member of parliament is the nation. The three or four hundred persons who may be present when a speech is delivered may be pleased or disgusted by the voice and action of the orator; but in the reports which are read the next day by hundreds of thousands, the difference between the noblest and the meanest figure, between the richest and the shrillest tones, between the most graceful and the most uncouth gesture, altogether vanishes. A hundred years ago, scarcely any report of what passed within the walls of the House of Commons was suffered to get abroad. In those times, therefore, the impression which a speaker might make on the persons who actually heard him was every thing. The impression out of doors was hardly worth a thought. In the parliaments of that time, therefore, as in the ancient commonwealths, those qualifications which enhance the immediate efforts of a speech, were far more important ingredients in the composition of an orator than they would appear to be in our time. All those qualifications Pitt possessed in the highest degree. On the stage, he would have been the finest Brutus or Coriolanus ever seen. Those who saw him in his decay, when his health was broken, when his mind was jangled, when he had been removed from that stormy assembly of which he thoroughly knew the temper, and over which he possessed unbounded influence, to a small, a torpid, and an unfriendly audience, say that his speaking was then for the most part a low monotonous muttering, audible only to those who sat close to him; that, when violently excited, he sometimes raised his voice for a few minutes, but that it soon sank again into an unintelligible murmur. Such was the Earl of Chatham; but such was not William Pitt. His figure, when he first appeared in parliament, was strikingly graceful and commanding, his features high and noble, his eye full of fire. His voice, even when it sank to a whisper, was heard to the remotest benches; when he strained it to its full extent, the sound rose like the swell of the organ of a great cathedral, shook the house with its peal, and was heard through lobbies and down staircases, to the Court of Requests and the precincts of Westminster Hall. He cultivated all these eminent advantages with the most assiduous care. His action is described, by a very malignant observer, as equal to that of Garrick. His play of countenance was wonderful; he frequently disconcerted a hostile orator by a single glance of indignation or scorn. Every tone, from the impassioned cry to the thrilling aside, was perfectly at his command. It is by no means improbable that the pains which he took to improve his great personal advantages, had in some respects a prejudicial operation, and tended to nourish in him that passion for theatrical effect which was one of the most conspicuous blemishes in his character.

"But it was not solely or principally to outward accomplishments that Pitt owed the vast influence which, during nearly thirty years, he exercised over the House of Commons. He was undoubtedly a great orator; and from the descriptions of his contemporaries, and the fragments of his speeches which still remain, it is not difficult to discover the nature and extent of his oratorical powers.

"He was no speaker of set speeches. His few prepared discourses were complete failures. The elaborate panegyric which he pronounced on General Wolfe was considered as the very worst of all his performances. 'No man,' says a critic who had often heard him, 'ever knew so little what he was going to say.' Indeed, his facility amounted to a vice; he was not the master, but the slave of his own speech. So little self-command had he when once he felt the impulse, that he did not like to take part in a debate when his mind was full of an important secret of state. 'I must sit still,' he once said to Lord Shelburne on such an occasion, 'for when once I am up, every thing that is in my mind comes out.'

"Yet he was not a great debater. That he should not have been so when he first entered the House of Commons, is not strange; scarcely any person has ever become so without long practice and many failures. It was by slow degrees, as Burke said, that Mr. Fox became the most brilliant and powerful debater that parliament ever saw. Mr. Fox himself attributed his own success to the resolution which he formed when very young, of speaking, well or ill, at least once every night. 'During five whole sessions,' he used to say, 'I spoke every night but one; and I regret only that I did not speak that night too.' Indeed, it would be difficult to name any great debater who has not made himself a master of his art at the expense of his audience.

"But as this art is one which even the ablest men have seldom acquired without long practice, so it is one which men of respectable abilities, with assiduous and intrepid practice, seldom fail to acquire. It is singular that, in such an art, Pitt, a man of splendid talents, great fluency, and dauntless boldness, whose whole life was passed in parliamentary conflicts, and who during several years was the leading minister of the Crown in the House of Commons, should never have attained to high excellence. He spoke without premeditation; but his speech followed the course of his own thoughts, and not that of the previous discussion. He could, indeed, treasure up in his memory some detached expression of a hostile orator, and make it the text for sparkling ridicule or burning invective.

Some of the most celebrated bursts of his eloquence were called forth by an unguarded word, a laugh, or a cheer. But this was the only sort of reply in which he appears to have excelled. He was perhaps the only great English orator who did not think it an advantage to have the last word, and who generally spoke by choice before his most formidable opponents. His merit was almost entirely rhetorical. He did not succeed either in exposition or refutation; but his speeches abounded with lively illustrations, striking apothegms, well-told anecdotes, happy allusions, passionate appeals. His invective and sarcasm were tremendous. Perhaps no English orator was ever so much feared.

"But that which gave most effect to his declamation was the air of sincerity, of vehement feeling, or moral elevation, which belonged to all that he said. His style was not always in the purest taste. Several contemporary judges pronounced it too florid. Walpole, in the midst of the rapturous eulogy which he pronounces on one of Pitt's greatest orations, owns that some of the metaphors were too forced. The quotations and classical stories of the orator are sometimes too trite for a clever schoolboy. But these were niceties for which the audience cared little. The enthusiasm of the orator infected all who were near him; his ardor and his noble bearing put fire into the most frigid conceit, and gave dignity to the most puerile allusion."

Such is the character of this great statesman and orator, as drawn by one masterly hand. It may perhaps both instruct and interest our readers if we present another, delineated by an artist equally distinguished for the vigor, judgment, and fidelity with which he paints such grand pieces for the gallery of history. The preceding, as we have already said, is from the pen of Lord Macaulay; the following is understood to be from that of Lord Brougham:

"The first place among the great qualities which distinguished Lord Chatham is unquestionably due to firmness of purpose, resolute determination in the pursuit of his objects. This was the characteristic of the younger Brutus, as he said, who had spared his life to fall by his hand—*Quicquid vult, id valde vult;* and although extremely apt to be shown in excess, it must be admitted to be the foundation of all true greatness of character. Every thing, however, depends upon the endowments in whose company it is found; and in Lord Chatham these were of a very high order. The quickness with which he could ascertain his object, and discover his road to it, was fully commensurate with his perseverance and his boldness in pursuing it; the firmness of grasp with which he held his advantage was fully equalled by the rapidity of the glance with which he discovered it. Add to this a mind eminently fertile in resources, a courage which nothing could daunt in the choice of his means, a resolution equally indomitable in their application, a genius, in short, original and daring, which bounded over the petty obstacles raised by ordinary men—their squeamishness, and their precedents, and their forms, and their regularities —and forced away its path through the entanglements of this base undergrowth to the worthy object ever in his view, the prosperity and the renown of his country. Far superior to the paltry objects of a grovelling ambition, and regardless alike of party and of personal considerations, he constantly set before his eyes the highest duty of a public man, to further the interests of his species. In pursuing his course towards that goal, he disregarded alike the frowns of power and the gales of popular applause; exposed himself undaunted to the vengeance of the court, while he battled against its corruptions, and confronted, unabashed, the rudest shocks of public indignation, while he resisted the dictates of pernicious agitators; and could conscientiously exclaim, with an illustrious statesman of antiquity, 'Ego hoc animo semper fui ut invidiam virtute partam, gloriam non invidium putarem.'

"Nothing could be more entangled than the foreign policy of this country at the time when he took the supreme direction of her affairs; nothing could be more disastrous than the aspect of her fortunes in every quarter of the globe. With a single ally in Europe, the King of Prussia, and him beset by a combination of all the continental powers in unnatural union to effect his destruction; with an army of insignificant amount, and commanded by men only desirous of grasping at the emoluments, without doing the duties or incurring the risks of their profession: with a navy that could hardly keep the sea, and whose chiefs vied with their comrades on shore in earning the character given them by the new minister, of being utterly unfit to be trusted in any enterprise accompanied with 'the least appearance of danger;' with a generally prevailing dislike of both services, which at once repressed all desire of joining either, and damped all public spirit in the country, by extinguishing all hope of success, and even all love of glory; it was hardly possible for a nation to be placed in circumstances more inauspicious to military exertions; and yet war raged in every quarter of the world where our dominion extended, while the territories of our only ally, as well as those of our own sovereign in Germany, were invaded by France, and her forces by sea and land menaced our shores. In the distant possessions of the Crown the same want of enterprise and of spirit prevailed. Armies in the West were paralyzed by the inaction of a captain who would hardly take the pains to write a despatch recording the nonentity of his operations; and in the East, while frightful disasters were brought upon our settlements by barbarian powers, the only military capacity that appeared in their defence was the accidental display of genius and valor by a merchant's clerk, who thus raised himself to celebrity (Mr., afterwards Lord, Clive). In this forlorn state of affairs, rendering it as impossible to think of peace as it seemed hopeless to continue the yet inevitable war, the base and sordid views of politicians kept pace with the mean spirit of the military caste; and parties were split or united, not upon any difference or agreement of public principle, but upon mere questions of patronage and share in the public spoil, while all seemed alike actuated by one only passion, the thirst alternately of power and of gain.

"As soon as Mr. Pitt took the helm, the steadiness of the hand that held it came to be felt in every motion of the vessel. There was no more of wavering councils, of torpid inaction, of listless expectancy, of abject despondency. His firmness gave confidence, his spirit roused courage, his vigilance secured exertion, in every department under his sway. Each man, from the first lord of the Admiralty down to the most humble clerk in the victualling office

—each soldier, from the commander-in-chief to the most obscure contractor or commissary—now felt assured that he was acting or indolent under the eye of one who knew his duties and his means as well as his own, and who would very certainly make all defaulters, whether through misfeasance or through nonfeasance, accountable for whatever detriment the commonwealth might sustain at their hands. Over his immediate coadjutors his influence swiftly obtained an ascendent which it ever after retained uninterrupted. Upon his first proposition for changing the conduct of the war he stood single among his colleagues, and tendered his resignation should they persist in their dissent; they at once succumbed, and from that hour ceased to have an opinion of their own upon any branch of the public affairs. Nay, so absolutely was he determined to have the control of those measures of which he knew the responsibility rested upon him alone, that he insisted upon the first lord of the Admiralty not having the correspondence of his own department; and no less eminent a naval character than Lord Anson, with his junior lords, were obliged to sign the orders issued by Mr. Pitt while the writing was covered over from their eyes.

"The effects of this change in the whole management of the public business, and in all the plans of the government, as well as in their execution, were speedily made manifest to all the world. The German troops were sent home, and a well-regulated militia being established to defend the country, a large disposable force was distributed over the various points whence the enemy might be annoyed. France, attacked on some points, and menaced on others, was compelled to retire from

Germany, soon afterwards suffered the most disastrous defeats, and, instead of threatening England and her allies with invasion, had to defend herself against attack, suffering severely in several of her most important naval stations. No less than sixteen islands, and settlements, and fortresses of importance, were taken from her in America, and Asia, and Africa, including all her West Indian colonies except St. Domingo, and all her settlements in the East. The whole important province of Canada was likewise conquered, and the Havana was taken from Spain. Besides this, the seas were swept clear of the fleets that had so lately been insulting all our colonies, and even all our coasts. Many general actions were fought and gained; one among them the most decisive that had ever been fought by our navy. Thirty-six sail of the line were taken or destroyed, fifty frigates, forty-five sloops of war. So brilliant a course of uninterrupted success had never in modern times attended the arms of any nation carrying on war with other states equal to it in civilization, and nearly a match in power. But it is a more glorious feature in the unexampled administration which history has to record, when it adds, that all public distress had disappeared; all discontent in any quarter, both of the colonies and parent state, had ceased; that no oppression was anywhere practised, no abuse suffered to prevail; that no encroachments were made upon the rights of the subject, no malversations tolerated in the possessors of power; and that England, for the first time and for the last time, presented the astonishing picture of a nation supporting without murmur a widely extended and costly war, and a people hitherto torn with conflicting parties so united in the service of the commonwealth, that the voice of faction had ceased in the land, and any discordant whisper was heard no more. 'These,' said the son of his first and most formidable adversary, Walpole, when informing his correspondent abroad that the session, as usual, had ended without any kind of opposition, or even of debate,—'these are the doings of Mr. Pitt, and they are wondrous in our eyes.'

"To genius irregularity is incident, and the greatest genius is often marked by eccentricity, as if it disdained to move in the vulgar orbit. Hence he who is fitted by his nature, and trained by his habits, to be an accomplished 'pilot in extremity,' and whose inclinations carry him forth to seek the deep when the waves run high, may be found, if not 'to steer too near the shore,' yet to despise the sunken rocks which they that can only be trusted in calm weather would have more surely avoided. To this rule it cannot be said that Lord Chatham afforded any exception; and, although a plot had certainly been formed to eject him from the ministry, leaving the chief control of affairs in the feeble hands of Lord Bute, whose only support was court favor, and whose only talent lay in an expertness at intrigue, yet there can be little doubt that this scheme was only rendered practicable by the hostility which the great minister's unbending habits, his contempt of ordinary men, and his neglect of everyday matters, had raised against him among all the creatures both of Downing Street and St. James's. In fact his colleagues, who necessarily felt humbled by his superiority, were needlessly mortified by the constant display of it;

and it would have betokened a still higher reach of understanding, as well as a purer fabric of patriotism, if he whose great capacity threw those subordinates into the shade, and before whose vigor in action they were sufficiently willing to yield, had united a little suavity in his demeanor with his extraordinary powers, nor made it always necessary for them to acknowledge as well as to feel their inferiority. It is certain that the insulting arrangement of the Admiralty to which reference has been already made, while it lowered that department in the public opinion, rendered all connected with him his personal enemies; and, indeed, though there have since his days been prime ministers whom he would never have suffered to sit even as puny lords at his boards, yet were one like himself again to govern the country, the Admiralty chief, who might be far inferior to Lord Anson, would never submit to the humiliation inflicted upon that gallant and skilful captain. Mr. Pitt's policy seemed formed upon the assumption that either each public functionary was equal to himself in boldness, activity, and resource, or that he was to preside over and animate each department in person ; and his confidence was such in his own powers that he reversed the maxim of governing, never to force your way where you can win it, and always disdained to insinuate where he could dash in, or to persuade where he could command. It thus happened that his colleagues were but nominally coadjutors, and though they durst not thwart him, yet rendered no heart-service to aid his schemes. Indeed, it has clearly appeared since his time that they were chiefly induced to yield him implicit obedience, and leave the undivided direction of all operations in his hands, by the expectation that the failure of what they were wont to sneer at as 'Mr. Pitt's visions,' would turn the tide of public opinion against him, and prepare his downfall from a height of which they felt that there was no one but himself able to dispossess him."

The same powerful writer, having thus sketched the character of the statesman, proceeds next to delineate that of the orator, as far as this can now be done from the extremely scanty and imperfect materials which have been preserved. The fame of Lord Chatham's eloquence is, in truth, almost wholly traditional.

"There is, indeed, hardly any eloquence, of ancient or of modern times, of which so little that can be relied on as authentic has been preserved; unless perhaps that of Pericles, Julius Cæsar, and Lord Bolingbroke. Of the actions of the two first we have sufficient records, as we have of Lord Chatham's; of their speeches we have little that can be regarded as genuine; although, by unquestionable tradition, we know that each of them was second only to the greatest orator of their respective countries; while of Bolingbroke we only know, from Dean Swift, that he was the most accomplished speaker of his time; and it is related of Mr. Pitt (the younger), that when the conversation rolled upon lost works, and some said they should prefer restoring the books of Livy, some of Tacitus, and some a Latin tragedy, he at once decided for a speech of Bolingbroke. What we know of his own father's oratory is much more to be gleaned from contemporary panegyrics, and accounts of its effects, than from the scanty, and for the most part doubtful, remains which have reached us.

"All accounts, however, concur in representing those effects to have been prodigious. The spirit and vehemence which animated its greater passages, their perfect application to the subject-matter of debate, the appositeness of his invective to the individual assailed, the boldness of the feats which he ventured upon, the grandeur of the ideas which he unfolded, the heart-stirring nature of his appeals, are all confessed by the united testimony of all his contemporaries; and the fragments which remain bear out to a considerable extent such representations; nor are we likely to be misled by those fragments, for the more striking portions were certainly the ones least likely to be either forgotten or fabricated. To these mighty attractions was added the imposing, the animating, the commanding power of a countenance singularly expressive; an eye so piercing that hardly any one could stand its glare; and a manner altogether singularly striking, original, and characteristic, notwithstanding a peculiarly defective and even awkward action. Latterly, indeed, his infirmities precluded all action; and he is described as standing in the House of Lords, leaning upon his crutch, and speaking for ten minutes together in an under-tone of voice scarcely audible, but raising his notes to their full pitch when he broke out into one of his grand bursts of invective or exclamation. But in his earlier time, his whole manner is represented as having been beyond conception animated and imposing. Indeed, the things which he effected by it principally, or at least which nothing but a most striking and commanding tone could have made it possible to attempt, almost exceed belief. Some of these sallies are indeed examples of that approach made to the ludicrous by the sublime, which has been charged upon him as a prevailing fault, and represented under the name of *charlatanerie*,—a favorite phrase with his adversaries, as it in later times has been with the ignorant undervaluers of Lord Erskine. It is related that once in the House of Commons he began a speech with the words, 'Sugar, Mr. Speaker,'—and then, observing a smile to prevail in the audience, he paused, looking fiercely around, and with a loud voice, rising in its notes, and swelling into vehement anger, he is said to have pronounced again the word 'Sugar!' three times, —and having thus quelled the house, and extinguished every appearance of levity or laughter, turned round, and disdainfully asked, 'Who will laugh at sugar now?' We have this anecdote on good traditional authority; that it was believed by those who had the best means of knowing Lord Chatham, is certain; and this of itself shows their sense of the extraordinary powers of his manner, and the reach of his audacity in trusting to those powers.

"There can be no doubt that of reasoning,—of sustained and close argument,—his speeches had but little. His statements were desultory though striking, perhaps not very distinct, certainly not all detailed, and as certainly every way inferior to those of his celebrated son. If he did not reason cogently, he assuredly did not compress his matter vigorously. He was any thing rather than a concise or a short speaker; not that his great passages were at all diffuse, or in the least degree loaded with superfluous words; but he was prolix in the whole texture of his discourse, and he was certainly the first who introduced into our senate the practice, adopted in the American war by Mr. Burke, and continued by others, of long speeches,—speeches of two and three hours, by which oratory has gained little and business less. His discourse was, however, fully informed with matter—his allusions to analogous subjects, and his reference to the history of past events, were frequent—his expression of his own opinions was copious and free, and stood very generally in the place of any elaborate reasoning in their support. A noble statement of enlarged views, a generous avowal of dignified sentiments, a manly and somewhat severe contempt for all petty or mean views, whether their baseness proceeded from narrow understanding or from corrupt bias, always pervaded his whole discourse; and, more than any other orator since Demosthenes, he was distinguished by the nobleness of feeling with which he regarded, and the amplitude of survey which he cast upon, the subject-matters of debate. His invective was unsparing and hard to be endured, although he was a less eminent master of sarcasm than his son, and rather overwhelmed his antagonist with the burst of words and vehement indignation, than wounded him by the edge of ridicule, or tortured him with the gall of bitter scorn, or fixed his arrow in the wound by the barb of epigram. These things seemed as it were to betoken too much labor and too much art; more labor than was consistent with absolute scorn, more art than could stand with heartfelt rage, or entire contempt inspired by the occasion, at the moment and on the spot. But his great passages,—those by which he has come down to us, those which gave his eloquence its peculiar character, and to which its dazzling success was owing,—were as sudden and unexpected as they were natural. Every one was taken by surprise when they rolled forth; every one felt them to be so natural that he could hardly understand why he had not thought of them himself, although into no one's imagination had they ever entered. If the quality of being natural without being obvious is a pretty correct description of felicitous expression, or what is called fine writing, it is a yet more accurate representation of fine passages or felicitous *hits* in speaking. In these all popular assemblies take boundless delight; by these, above all others, are the minds of an audience at pleasure moved or controlled. They form the grand charm of Lord Chatham's oratory; they were the distinguishing excellence of his great predecessor, and gave him at will to wield the fierce democracy of Athens, and to fulmine over Greece."

Many years ago, a small volume was

published by Lord Grenville, containing letters written by the Earl of Chatham to his nephew Thomas Pitt, Lord Camelford. They are replete with ex cellent advice, conveyed in an easy, affectionate, and not inelegant style, having all of them been penned evidently without effort, under the simple impulse of the kindly feelings and anxious interest which they manifest throughout. At the same time, they might have been written by a person vastly inferior to Lord Chatham; and indeed one can scarcely avoid surprise at the absence of every trace of that genius, power, and originality for which the writer was so greatly distinguished.

Almon, the bookseller, has written *Anecdotes of the Life of the Earl of Chatham*, 3 vols. 8vo.; the Rev. Mr. Thackeray has illustrated the subject more accurately, as well as fully, in his *History of the Earl of Chatham*, 2 vols.

4to. None of his own writings have been given to the world, except a small volume of letters to the son of his elder brother, afterwards Lord Camelford, published some years ago by Lord Grenville; and his *Correspondence,* in 4 vols. 8vo., 1838–40. The *Correspondence* illustrates very fully his life and character, and furnishes valuable materials for the political history of his time. His wife, who died in 1803, bore him three sons and two daughters. The second son, the subject of the next article, gained a political fame capable of rivalling that of his illustrious father.

WILLIAM PITT.

William Pitt, the second son of William Pitt, Earl of Chatham, and of Lady Hester Grenville, daughter of Hester, Countess Temple, was born on the 28th of May, 1759. The child inherited a name which, at the time of his birth, was the most illustrious in the civilized world, and was pronounced by every Englishman with pride, and by every enemy of England with mingled admiration and terror. During the first year of his life, every month had its illuminations and bonfires, and every wind brought some messenger charged with joyful tidings and hostile standards. In Westphalia the English infantry won a great battle which arrested the armies of Louis the Fifteenth in the midst of a career of conquest: Boscawen defeated one French fleet on the coast of Portugal: Hawke put to flight another in the Bay of Biscay: Johnson took Niagara: Amherst took Ticonderoga: Wolfe died by the most enviable of deaths under the walls of Quebec: Clive destroyed a Dutch armament in the Hoogley, and established the English supremacy in Bengal: Coote routed Lally at Wandewash, and established the English supremacy in the Carnatic. The nation, while loudly applauding the successful warriors, considered them all, on sea and on land, in Europe, in America, and in Asia, merely as instruments which received their direction from one superior mind. It was the great William Pitt, the great commoner, who had vanquished French marshals in Germany, and French admirals on the Atlantic; who had conquered for his country one great empire on the frozen shores of Ontario, and another under the tropical sun near the mouths of the Ganges. It was not in the nature of things that popularity such as he at this time enjoyed should be permanent. That popularity had lost its gloss before his children were old enough to understand that their father was a great man. He was at length placed in situations in which neither his talents for administration nor his talents for debate appeared to the best advantage. The energy and decision which had eminently fitted him for the direction of war were not needed in time of peace. The lofty and spirit-stirring eloquence, which had made him supreme in the House of Commons, often fell dead on the House of Lords. A cruel malady racked his joints, and left his joints only to fall on his nerves and on his brain. During the closing years of his life, he was odious to the court, and yet was not on cordial terms with the great body of the opposition. Chatham was only the ruin of Pitt, but an awful and majestic ruin, not to be contemplated by any man of sense and feeling without emotions resembling those which are excited by the remains of the Parthenon and of the Coliseum. In one respect the old statesman was eminently happy. Whatever might be the vicissitudes of his public life, he never failed to find peace and love by his own hearth. He loved all his children, and was loved by them; and, of all his children, the one of whom he was fondest and proudest was his second son.

The child's genius and ambition displayed themselves with a rare and almost unnatural precocity. At seven, the interest which he took in grave subjects, the ardor with which he pursued his studies, and the sense and vivacity of his remarks on books and on events, amazed his parents and instructors. One of his sayings of this date was reported to his mother by his tutor. In August, 1776, when the world was agitated by the news that Mr. Pitt had become Earl of Chatham, little William exclaimed, "I am glad that I am not the eldest son. I want to speak in the House of Commons like papa." A letter is extant in which Lady Chatham, a woman of considerable abilities, remarked to her lord, that their younger son at twelve had left far behind him his elder brother, who was fifteen. "The fineness," she wrote, "of William's mind, makes him enjoy with the greatest pleasure what would be above the reach of any other creature of his small age." At fourteen the lad was in intellect a man. Hayley, who met him at Lyme in the summer of 1773, was astonished, delighted, and somewhat overawed, by hearing wit and wisdom from so young a mouth. The poet, indeed, was afterwards sorry that his shyness had prevented him from submitting the plan of an extensive literary work, which he was then meditating, to the judgment of this extraordinary boy. The boy, indeed, had already written a tragedy, bad of course, but not worse than the tragedies of his friend. This piece is still preserved at Chevening, and is in some respects highly curious. There is no love. The whole plot is political; and it is remarkable that the interest, such as it is, turns on a contest about a regency. On one side is a faithful servant of the Crown, on the other an ambitious and unprincipled conspirator. At length the King, who had been missing, reappears, resumes his power, and rewards the faithful defender of his rights. A reader who should judge only by internal evidence, would have no hesitation in pronouncing that the play was written by some Pittite poetaster at the time of the rejoicings for the recovery of George the Third in 1789.

The pleasure with which William's parents observed the rapid development of his intellectual powers was alloyed by apprehensions about his health. He shot up alarmingly fast; he was often ill, and always weak; and it was feared that it would be impossible to rear a stripling so tall, so slender, and so feeble. Port wine was prescribed by his medical advisers; and it is said that he was, at fourteen, accustomed to take this agreeable physic in quantities which would, in our abstemious age, be thought much more than sufficient for any full-grown man. This regimen, though it would probably have killed ninety-nine boys out of a hundred, seems to have been well suited to the peculiarities of William's constitution; for at fifteen he ceased to be molested by disease, and, though never a strong man, continued, during many years of labor and anxiety, of nights passed in debate and of summers passed in London, to be a tolerably healthy one. It was probably on account of the delicacy of his frame that he was not educated like other boys of the same rank. Almost all the eminent English statesmen and orators to whom he was afterwards opposed or allied, North, Fox, Shelburne, Windham, Grey, Wellesley, Grenville, Sheridan, Canning, went through the training of great public schools. Lord Chatham had himself been a distinguished Etonian; and it is seldom that a distinguished Etonian forgets his obligations to Eton. But William's infirmities required a vigilance and tenderness such as could be found only at home. He was therefore bred under the paternal roof. His studies were superintended by a clergyman named Wilson; and those studies, though often interrupted by illness, were prosecuted with extraordinary success. Before the lad had completed his fifteenth year, his knowledge both of the ancient languages and of mathematics was such as very few men of eighteen then carried up to college. He was therefore sent, towards the close of the year 1773, to Pembroke Hall, in the university of Cambridge. So young a student required much more than the ordinary care which a college tutor bestows on undergraduates. The governor, to whom the direction of William's academical life was confided, was a bachelor of arts named Pretyman, who had been senior wrangler in the preceding year, and who, though not a man of prepossessing appearance or brilliant parts, was eminently acute and laborious, a sound scholar, and an excellent geometrician. At Cambridge, Pretyman was, during more than two years, the inseparable companion, and indeed almost the only companion, of his pupil. A close and lasting friendship sprang up between the pair. The disciple was able, before he completed his twenty-eighth year, to make his preceptor bishop of Lincoln and dean of St. Paul's; and the preceptor showed his gratitude by writing a Life of the disciple, which enjoys the distinction of being the worst biographical work of its size in the world.

Pitt, till he graduated, had scarcely one acquaintance, attended chapel regularly morning and evening, dined every day in hall, and never went to a single evening party. At seventeen, he was admitted, after the bad fashion of those times, by right of birth, without any examination, to the degree of Master of Arts. But he continued during some years to reside at college, and to apply himself vigorously, under Pretyman's direction, to the studies of the place, while mixing freely in the best academic society.

The stock of learning which Pitt laid in during this part of his life was certainly very extraordinary. In fact, it was all that he ever possessed; for he very early became too busy to have any spare time for books. The work in which he took the greatest delight was Newton's Principia. His liking for mathematics, indeed, amounted to a passion, which, in the opinion of his instructors, themselves distinguished mathematicians, required to be checked rather than encouraged. The acuteness and readiness with which he solved problems was pronounced by one of the ablest of the moderators, who in those days presided over the disputations in the schools, and conducted the examinations of the Senate-House, to be unrivalled in the university. Nor was the youth's proficiency in classical learning less remarkable. In one respect, indeed, he appeared to disadvantage when compared with even second-rate and third-rate men from public schools. He had never, while under Wilson's care, been in the habit of composing in the ancient languages; and he therefore never acquired that knack of versification which is sometimes possessed by clever boys whose knowledge of the language and literature of Greece and Rome is very superficial. It would have been utterly out of his power to produce such charming elegiac lines as those in which Wellesley bade farewell to Eton, or such Virgilian hexameters as those in which Canning described the pilgrimage to Mecca. But it may be doubted whether any scholar has ever, at twenty, had a more solid and profound knowledge of the two great tongues of the old civilized world. The facility with which he penetrated the meaning of the most intricate sentences in the At[illegible] writers astonished veteran critics. [illegible] had set his heart on being inti[illegible]ely acquainted with all the extant [illegible]ry of Greece, and was not satisfied t[illegible] had mastered Lycophron's Cassandra, the most obscure work in the whole range of ancient literature. This strange rhapsody, the difficulties of which have perplexed and repelled many excellent scholars, "he read," says his preceptor, "with an ease at first, which, if I had not witnessed it, I should have thought beyond the compass of human intellect."

To modern literature Pitt paid comparatively little attention. He knew no living language except French; and French he knew very imperfectly. With a few of the best English writers he was intimate, particularly with Shakspeare and Milton. The debate in Pandemonium was, as it well deserved to be, one of his favorite passages; and his early friends used to ta[illegible] long after his death, of the just [illegible] phasis and the melodious cadence w[illegible] which they had heard him recite t[illegible] incomparable speech of Belial. He had indeed been carefully trained from infancy in the art of managing his voice, a voice naturally clear and deeptoned. His father, whose oratory owed no small part of its effect to that art, had been a most skilful and judicious instructor. At a later period, the wits of Brookes's, irritated by observing, night after night, how powerfully Pitt's sonorous elocution fascinated the rows of country gentlemen, reproached him with having been "taught by his dad on a stool."

His education, indeed, was well adapted to form a great parliamentary speaker. One argument often urged against those classical studies which occupy so large a part of the early life of every gentleman bred in the south of our island is, that they prevent him from acquiring a command of his mother tongue, and that it is not unusual to meet with a youth of excellent parts, who writes Ciceronian Latin prose and Horatian Latin Alcaics, but who would find it impossible to express his thoughts in pure, perspicuous, and forcible English. There may perhaps be some truth in this observation. But the classical studies of Pitt were carried on in a peculiar manner, and had the effect of enriching his English vocabulary, and of making him wonderfully expert in the art of constructing correct English sentences. His practice was to look over a page or two of a Greek or Latin author, to make himself master of the meaning, and then to read the passage straight forward into his own language. This practice, begun under his first teacher Wilson, was continued under Pretyman. It is not strange that a young man of great abilities, who had been exercised daily in this way during ten years, should have acquired an almost unrivalled power of putting his thoughts, without premeditation, into words well selected and well arranged.

Of all the remains of antiquity, the orations were those on which he bestowed the most minute examination.

His favorite employment was to compare harangues on opposite sides of the same question, to analyze them, and to observe which of the arguments of the first speaker were refuted by the second, which were evaded, and which were left untouched. Nor was it only in books that he at this time studied the art of parliamentary fencing. When he was at home, he had frequent opportunities of hearing important debates at Westminster; and he heard them, not only with interest and enjoyment, but with a close scientific attention, resembling that with which a diligent pupil at Guy's Hospital watches every turn of the hand of a great surgeon through a difficult operation. On one of these occasions, Pitt, a youth whose abilities were as yet known only to his own family and to a small knot of college friends, was introduced on the steps of the throne in the House of

Lords to Fox, who was his senior by eleven years, and who was already the greatest debater, and one of the greatest orators, that had appeared in England. Fox used afterwards to relate that, as the discussion proceeded, Pitt repeatedly turned to him, and said, "But surely, Mr. Fox, that might be met thus;" or, "Yes; but he lays himself open to this retort." What the particular criticisms were, Fox had forgotten; but he said that he was much struck at the time by the precocity of a lad who, through the whole sitting, seemed to be thinking only how all the speeches on both sides could be answered.

One of the young man's visits to the House of Lords was a sad and memorable era in his life. He had not quite completed his nineteenth year, when, on the 7th of April, 1778, he attended his father to Westminster. A great debate was expected. It was known that France had recognized the independence of the United States. The Duke of Richmond was about to declare his opinion that all thought of subjugating those states ought to be relinquished. Chatham had always maintained that the resistance of the colonies to the mother country was justifiable. But he conceived, very erroneously, that on the day on which their independence should be acknowledged the greatness of England would be at an end. Though sinking under the weight of years and infirmities, he determined, in spite of the entreaties of his family, to be in his place. His son supported him to a seat. The excitement and exertion were too much for the old man. In the very act of addressing the peers, he fell back in convulsions. A few weeks later his corpse was borne, with gloomy pomp, from the Painted

6

Chamber to the Abbey. The favorite child and namesake of the deceased statesman followed the coffin as chief mourner, and saw it deposited in the transept where his own was destined to lie.

His elder brother, now Earl of Chatham, had means sufficient, and barely sufficient, to support the dignity of the peerage. The other members of the family were poorly provided for. William had little more than three hundred a-year. It was necessary for him to follow a profession. He had already begun to eat his terms. In the spring of 1780 he came of age. He then quitted Cambridge, was called to the bar, took chambers in Lincoln's Inn, and joined the western circuit. In the autumn of that year a general election took place; and he offered himself as a candidate for the university; but he was at the bottom of the poll. It is said that the grave doctors who then sat, robed in scarlet, on the benches of Golgotha, thought it great presumption in so young a man to solicit so high a distinction. He was, however, at the request of a hereditary friend, the Duke of Rutland, brought into parliament by Sir James Lowther for the borough of Appleby.

The dangers of the country were at that time such as might well have disturbed even a constant mind. Army after army had been sent in vain against the rebellious colonists of North America. On pitched fields of battle the advantage had been with the disciplined troops of the mother country. But it was not on pitched fields of battle that the event of such a contest could be decided. An armed nation, with hunger and the Atlantic for auxiliaries, was not to be subjugated. Meanwhile, the House of Bourbon, humbled to the dust a few years before by the genius and vigor of Chatham, had seized the opportunity of revenge. France and Spain were united against us, and had recently been joined by Holland. The command of the Mediterranean had been for a time lost. The British flag had been scarcely able to maintain itself in the British Channel. The northern powers professed neutrality; but their neutrality had a menacing aspect. In the East, Hyder had descended on the Carnatic, had destroyed the little army of Baillie, and had spread terror even to the ramparts of Fort Saint George. The discontents of Ireland threatened nothing less than civil war. In England the authority of the government had sunk to the lowest point. The King and the House of Commons were alike unpopular. The cry for parliamentary reform was scarcely less loud and vehement than in the autumn of 1830. Formidable associations, headed, not by ordinary demagogues, but by men of high rank, stainless character, and distinguished ability, demanded a revision of the representative system. The populace, emboldened by the impotence and irresolution of the government, had recently broken loose from all restraint, besieged the chambers of the legislature, hustled peers, hunted bishops, attacked the residences of ambassadors, opened prisons, burned and pulled down houses. London had presented during some days the aspect of a city taken by storm; and it had been necessary to form a camp among the trees of St. James's Park.

In spite of dangers and difficulties, abroad and at home, George the Third, with a firmness which had little affinity with virtue or with wisdom, persisted in his determination to put down the American rebels by force of arms; and his ministers submitted their judgment to his. Some of them were probably actuated merely by selfish cupidity, but their chief, Lord North, a man of high honor, amiable temper, winning manners, lively wit, and excellent talents both for business and for debate, must be acquitted of all sordid motives. He remained at a post from which he had long wished and had repeatedly tried to escape, only because he had not sufficient fortitude to resist the entreaties and reproaches of the King, who silenced all arguments by passionately asking whether any gentleman, any man of spirit, could have the heart to desert a kind master in the hour of extremity.

The opposition consisted of two parties which had once been hostile to each other, and which had been very slowly, and, as it soon appeared, very imperfectly reconciled, but which at this conjuncture seemed to act together with cordiality. The larger of these parties consisted of the great body of the Whig aristocracy. Its head was Charles, Marquis of Rockingham, a man of sense and virtue, and in wealth and parliamentary interest equalled by very few of the English nobles, but afflicted with a nervous timidity which prevented him from taking a prominent part in debate. In the House of Commons the adherents of Rockingham were led by Fox, whose dissipated habits and ruined fortunes were the talk of the whole town, but whose commanding genius, and whose sweet, generous, and affectionate disposition extorted the admiration and love of those who most lamented the errors of his private life. Burke, superior to Fox in largeness of comprehension, in extent of knowledge, and in splendor of imagination, but less skilled in that kind of logic and in that kind of rhetoric which convince and persuade great assemblies, was willing to be the lieutenant of a young chief who might have been his son.

A smaller section of the opposition was composed of the old followers of Chatham. At their head was William, Earl of Shelburne, distinguished both as a statesman and as a lover of science and letters. With him were leagued Lord Camden, who had formerly held the great seal, and whose integrity, ability, and constitutional knowledge commanded the public respect; Barré, an eloquent and acrimonious declaimer; and Dunning, who had long held the first place at the English bar. It was to this party that Pitt was naturally attracted.

On the 26th of February, 1781, he made his first speech in favor of Burke's plan of economical reform.

Fox stood up at the same moment, but instantly gave way. The lofty yet animated deportment of the young member, his perfect self-possession, the readiness with which he replied to the orators who had preceded him, the silver tones of his voice, the perfect structure of his unpremeditated sentences, astonished and delighted his hearers. Burke, moved even to tears, exclaimed, "It is not a chip of the old block; it is the old block itself." "Pitt will be one of the first men in parliament," said a member of the opposition to Fox. "He is so already," answered Fox, in whose nature envy had no place. It is a curious fact, well remembered by some who were very recently living, that soon after this debate Pitt's name was put up by Fox at Brookes's.

On two subsequent occasions during that session Pitt addressed the house, and on both fully sustained the reputation which he had acquired on his first appearance. In the summer, after the prorogation, he again went the western circuit, held several briefs, and acquitted himself in such a manner that he was highly complimented by Buller from the bench, and by Dunning at the bar.

On the 27th of November the parliament reassembled. Only forty-eight hours before had arrived tidings of the surrender of Cornwallis and his army; and it consequently became necessary to rewrite the royal speech. Every man in the kingdom, except the King, was now convinced that it was mere madness to think of conquering the United States. In the debate on the report of the address, Pitt spoke with even more energy and brilliancy than on any former occasion. He was warmly applauded by his allies; but it was remarked that no person on his own side of the house was so loud in eulogy as Henry Dundas, the Lord Advocate of Scotland, who spoke from the ministerial ranks. That able and versatile politician distinctly foresaw the approaching downfall of the government with which he was connected, and was preparing to make his own escape from the ruin. From that night dates his connection with Pitt, a connection which soon became a close intimacy, and which lasted till it was dissolved by death.

About a fortnight later, Pitt spoke in the committee of supply on the army estimates. Symptoms of dissension had begun to appear on the trea sury bench. Lord George Germaine, the secretary of state, who was especially charged with the direction of the war in America, had held language not easily to be reconciled with declarations made by the first lord of the treasury. Pitt noticed the discrepancy with much force and keenness. Lord George and Lord North began to whisper together; and Welbore Ellis, an ancient placeman, who had been drawing salary almost every quarter since the days of Henry Pelham, bent down between them to put in a word. Such interruptions sometimes discompose veteran speakers. Pitt stopped, and, looking at the group, said, with admirable readiness, "I shall wait till Nestor has composed the dispute between Agamemnon and Achilles."

After several defeats, or victories hardly to be distinguished from defeats, the ministry resigned. The King, reluctantly and ungraciously, consented to accept Rockingham as first minister. Fox and Shelburne became secretaries of state. Lord John Cavendish, one of the most upright and honorable of men, was made chancellor of the exchequer.

Thurlow, whose abilities and force of character had made him the dictator of the House of Lords, continued to hold the great seal.

To Pitt was offered, through Shelburne, the vice-treasurership of Ireland, one of the easiest and most highly paid places in the gift of the Crown ; but the offer was, without hesitation, declined. The young statesman had resolved to accept no post which did not entitle him to a seat in the cabinet; and, a few days later, he announced that resolution in the House of Commons. It must be remembered that the cabinet was then a much smaller and more select body than at present. We have seen cabinets of sixteen. In the time of our grandfathers a cabinet of ten or eleven was thought inconveniently large. Seven was a usual number. Even Burke, who had taken the lucrative office of paymaster, was not in the cabinet. Many therefore thought Pitt's declaration indecent. He himself was sorry that he had made it. The words, he said in private, had escaped him in the heat of speaking; and he had no sooner uttered them than he would have given the world to recall them. They, however, did him no harm with the public. The second William Pitt, it was said, had shown that he had inherited the spirit as well as the genius of the first. In the son, as in the father, there might perhaps be too much pride; but there was nothing low or sordid. It might be called arrogance in a young barrister, living in chambers on three hundred a year, to refuse a salary of five thousand a year, merely because he did not choose to bind himself to speak or vote for plans which he had no share in framing; but surely such arrogance was not very far removed from virtue.

Pitt gave a general support to the administration of Rockingham, but omitted, in the mean time, no opportunity of courting that ultra-whig party which the persecution of Wilkes and the Middlesex election had called into existence, and which the disastrous events of war, and the triumph of republican principles in America, had made formidable both in numbers and in temper. He supported a motion for shortening the duration of parliaments. He made a motion for a committee to examine into the state of the representation, and, in the speech by which that motion was introduced, avowed himself the enemy of the close boroughs, the strongholds of that corruption to which he attributed all the calamities of the nation, and which, as he phrased it in one of those exact and sonorons sentences of which he had a boundless command, had grown with the growth of England and strengthened with her strength, but had not diminished with her diminution, or decayed with her decay. On this occasion he was supported by Fox. The motion was lost by only twenty votes in a house of more than three hundred members. The reformers never again had so good a division till the year 1831.

The new administration was strong in abilities, and was more popular than any administration which had held office since the first year of George the Third, but was hated by the King, hesitatingly supported by the parliament, and torn by internal dissensions. The chancellor was disliked and distrusted by almost all his colleagues. The two secretares of state regarded each other with no friendly feeling. The line between their departments had not been traced with precision; and there were consequently jealousies, encroachments and complaints. It was all that Rockingham could do to keep the peace in his cabinet; and before the cabinet had existed three months, Rockingham died.

In an instant all was confusion. The adherents of the deceased statesman looked on the Duke of Portland as their chief. The King placed Shelburne at the head of the treasury. Fox, Lord John Cavendish, and Burke, immediately resigned their offices; and the new prime minister was left to constitute a government out of very defective materials. His own parliamentary talents were great; but he could not be in the place where parliamentary talents were most needed. It was necessary to find some member of the House of Commons who could confront the great orators of the opposition; and Pitt alone had the eloquence and the courage which were required. He was offered the great place of chancellor of the exchequer, and he accepted it. He had scarcely completed his twenty-third year.

The parliament was speedily prorogued. During the recess, a negotiation for peace which had been commenced under Rockingham was brought to a successful termination. England acknowledged the independence of her revolted colonies; and she ceded to her European enemies some places in the Mediterranean, and in the Gulf of Mexico. But the terms which she obtained were quite as advantageous and honorable as the events of the war entitled her to expect, or as she was likely to obtain by persevering in a contest against immense odds. All her vital parts, all the real sources of her power remained uninjured. She preserved even her dignity; for she ceded to the House of Bourbon only part of what she had won from that house in previous wars. She retained her Indian empire undiminished; and, in spité of the mightiest efforts of two great monarchies, her flag still waved on the rock of Gibraltar. There is not the slightest reason to believe that Fox, if he had remained in office, would have hesitated one moment about concluding a treaty on such conditions. Unhappily that great and most amiable man was, at this crisis, hurried by his passions into an error which made his genius and his virtues, during a long course of years, almost useless to his country.

He saw that the great body of the House of Commons was divided into three parties, his own, that of North, and that of Shelburne; that none of those three parties was large enough to stand alone; that, therefore, unless two of them united, there must be a miserably feeble administration, or, more probably, a rapid succession of miserably feeble administrations, and this at a time when a strong government was essential to the prosperity and respectability of the nation. It was then necessary and right that there should be a coalition. To every possible coalition there were objections. But, of all possible coalitions, that to which there were the fewest objections, was undoubtedly a coalition between Shelburne and Fox. It would have been generally applauded by the followers of both. It might have been made without any sacrifice of public principle on the part of either. Unhappily, recent bickerings had left in the mind of Fox a profound dislike and distrust of Shelburne. Pitt attempted to mediate, and was authorised to invite Fox to return to the service of the Crown. "Is Lord Shelburne," said Fox, "to remain prime minister?" Pitt answered in the affirmative. "It is impossible that I can act under him," said Fox. "Then negotiation is at an end," said Pitt; "for I cannot betray him." Thus the two statesmen parted. They were never again in a private room together.

As Fox and his friends would not treat with Shelburne, nothing remained to them but to treat with North. That fatal coalition, which is emphatically called "The Coalition," was formed. Not three quarters of a year had elapsed since Fox and Burke had threatened North with impeachment, and had described him, night after night, as the most arbitrary, the most corrupt, the most incapable of ministers. They now allied themselves with him for the purpose of driving from office a statesman with whom they cannot be said to have differed as to any important question. Nor had they even the prudence and the patience to wait for some occasion on which they might, without inconsistency, have combined with their old enemies in opposition to the government. That nothing might be wanting to the scandal, the great orators who had, during seven years, thundered against the war, determined to join with the authors of that war in passing a vote of censure on the peace.

The parliament met before Christmas 1782. But it was not till January 1783 that the preliminary treaties were signed. On the 17th of February they were taken into consideration by the House of Commons. There had been, during some days, floating rumors that Fox and North had coalesced; and the debate indicated but too clearly that those rumors were not unfounded. Pitt was suffering from indisposition: he did not rise till his own strength and that of his hearers were exhausted; and he was consequently less successful than on any former occasion. His admirers owned that his speech was feeble and petulant. He so far forgot himself as to advise Sheridan to confine himself to amusing theatrical audiences. This ignoble sarcasm gave Sheridan an opportunity of retorting with great felicity. "After what I have seen and heard to-night," he said, "I really feel strongly tempted to venture on a competition with so great an artist as Ben Jonson, and to bring on the stage a second Angry Boy." On a division, the address proposed by the supporters of the government was rejected by a majority of sixteen.

But Pitt was not a man to be disheartened by a single failure, or to be put down by the most lively repartee. When, a few days later, the opposition proposed a resolution directly censuring the treaties, he spoke with an eloquence, energy, and dignity, which raised his fame and popularity higher than ever. To the coalition of Fox and North he alluded in language which drew forth tumultuous applause from his followers. "If," he said, "this ill-omened and unnatural marriage be not yet consummated, I know of a just and lawful impediment; and, in the name of the public weal, I forbid the banns."

The ministers were again left in a minority, and Shelburne consequently tendered his resignation. It was accepted: but the King struggled long and hard before he submitted to the terms dictated by Fox, whose faults he detested, and whose high spirit and powerful intellect he detested still more. The first place at the board of treasury was repeatedly offered to Pitt: but the offer, though tempting, was steadfastly declined. The young man, whose judgment was as precocious as his eloquence, saw that his time was coming, but was not come, and was deaf to royal importunities and reproaches. His Majesty, bitterly complaining of Pitt's faintheartedness, tried to break the coalition. Every art of seduction was practised on North, but in vain. During several weeks the country remained without a government. It was not till all devices had failed, and till the aspect of the House of Commons became threatening, that the King gave way. The Duke of Portland was declared first lord of the treasury. Thurlow was dismissed. Fox and North became secretaries of state, with power ostensibly equal. But Fox was the real prime minister.

The year was far advanced before the new arrangements were completed; and nothing very important was done during the remainder of the session. Pitt, now seated on the opposition bench, brought the question of parliamentary reform a second time under the consideration of the Commons. He proposed to add to the house at once a hundred county members and several members for metropolitan districts, and to enact that every borough of which an election committee should report that the majority of voters appeared to be corrupt, should lose the franchise. The motion was rejected by 293 votes to 149.

After the prorogation, Pitt visited the Continent for the first and last time. His travelling companion was one of his most intimate friends, a young man of his own age, who had already distinguished himself in parliament by an engaging natural eloquence, set off by the sweetest and most exquisitely modulated of human voices, and whose affectionate heart, caressing manners, and brilliant wit, made him the most delightful of companions, William Wilberforce. That was the time of Anglomania in France; and at Paris the son of the great Chatham was absolutely hunted by men of letters and women of fashion, and forced, much against his will, into political disputation. One remarkable saying which dropped from him during this tour has been preserved. A French gentleman expressed some surprise at the immense influence which Fox, a man of pleasure, ruined by the dice-box and the turf, exercised over the English nation. "You have not," said Pitt, "been under the wand of the magician."

In November 1783 the parliament met again. The government had irresistible strength in the House of Commons, and seemed to be scarcely less strong in the House of Lords, but was, in truth, surrounded on every side by dangers. The King was impatiently waiting for the moment at which he could emancipate himself from a yoke which galled him so severely, that he had more than once seriously thought of retiring to Hanover; and the King was scarcely more eager for a change than the nation. Fox and North had committed a fatal error. They ought to have known that coalitions between parties which have long been hostile, can succeed only when the wish for coalition pervades the lower ranks of both. If the leaders unite before there is any disposition to union among the followers, the probability is that there will be a mutiny in both camps, and that the two revolted armies will make a truce with each other, in order to be revenged on those by whom they think that they have been betrayed. Thus it was in 1783. At the beginning of that eventful year, North had been the recognized head of the old Tory party, which, though for a moment prostrated by the disastrous issue of the American war, was still a great power in the state. To him the clergy, the universities, and that large body of country gentlemen whose rallying cry was "Church and King," had long looked up with respect and confidence. Fox had, on the other hand, been the idol of the Whigs, and of the whole body of Protestant dissenters. The coalition at once alienated the most zealous Tories from North, and the most zealous Whigs from Fox. The university of Oxford, which had marked its approbation of North's orthodoxy by electing him chancellor, the city of London, which had been, during two and twenty years, at war with the Court, were equally disgusted. Squires and rectors, who had inherited the principles of the cavaliers of the preceding century, could not forgive their old leader for combining with disloyal subjects in order to put a force on the sovereign. The members of the Bill of Rights Society and of the Reform Associations were enraged by learning that their favorite orator now called the great champion of tyranny and corruption his noble friend. Two great multitudes were at once left without any head, and both at once turned their eyes on Pitt. One party saw in him the only man who could rescue the King; the other saw in him the only man who could purify the parliament. He was supported on one side by Archbishop Markham, the preacher of divine right, and by Jenkinson, the captain of the Prætorian band of the King's friends; on the other side by Jebb and Priestley, Sawbridge and Cartwright, Jack Wilkes and Horne Tooke. On the benches of the House of Commons, however, the ranks of the ministerial majority were unbroken; and that any statesman would venture to brave such a majority was thought impossible. No prince of the Hanoverian line had ever, under any provocation, ventured to appeal from the representative body to the constituent body. The ministers, therefore, notwithstanding the sullen looks and muttered words of displeasure with which their suggestions were received in the closet, notwithstanding the roar of obloquy which was rising louder and louder every day from every corner of the island, thought themselves secure.

Such was their confidence in their strength that, as soon as the parliament had met, they brought forward a singularly bold and original plan for the government of the British territories in India. What was proposed was that the whole authority, which till that time had been exercised over those territories by the East India Company, should be transferred to seven commissioners, who were to be named by parliament, and were not to be removable at the pleasure of the Crown. Earl Fitzwilliam, the most intimate personal friend of Fox, was to be chairman of this board, and the eldest son of North was to be one of the members.

As soon as the outlines of the scheme were known, all the hatred which the coalition had excited burst forth with an astounding explosion. The question which ought undoubtedly to have been considered as paramount to every other was, whether the proposed change was likely to be beneficial or injurious to the thirty millions of people who were subject to the Company. But that question cannot be said to have been even seriously discussed. Burke, who, whether right or wrong in the conclusions to which he came, had at least the merit of looking at the subject in the right point of view, vainly reminded his hearers of that mighty population whose daily rice might depend on a vote of the British parliament. He spoke, with even more than his wonted power of thought and language, about the desolation of Rohilcund, about the spoliation of Benares, about the evil policy which had suffered the tanks of the Carnatic to go to ruin; but he could scarcely obtain a hearing. The contending parties, to their shame it must be said, would listen to none but English topics. Out of doors the cry against the ministry was almost universal. Town and country were united. Corporations exclaimed against the violation of the charter of the greatest corporation in the realm. Tories and democrats joined in pronouncing the proposed board an unconstitutional body. It was to consist of Fox's nominees. The effect of his bill was to give, not to the Crown, but to him personally, whether in office or in opposition, an enormous power, a patronage sufficient to counterbalance the patronage of the Treasury and of the Admiralty, and to decide the elections for fifty boroughs. He knew, it was said, that he was hateful alike to King and people; and he had devised a plan which would make him independent of both. Some nicknamed him Cromwell, and some Carlo Khan. Wilberforce, with his usual felicity of expression, and with very unusual bitterness of feeling, described the scheme as the genuine offspring of the coalition, as marked with the features of both its parents, the corruption of one and the violence of the other. In spite of all opposition, however, the bill was supported in every stage by great majorities, was rapidly passed, and was sent up to the Lords. To the general astonishment, when the second reading was moved in the upper house, the opposition proposed an adjournment, and carried it by eighty-seven votes to seventy-nine. The cause of this strange turn of fortune was soon known. Pitt's cousin, Earl Temple, had been in the royal closet, and had there been authorized to let it be known that his Majesty would consider all who voted for the bill as his enemies. The ignominious commission was performed, and instantly a troop of lords of the bedchamber, of bishops who wished to be translated, and of Scotch peers who who wished to be re-elected, made haste to change sides. On a later day, the Lords rejected the bill. Fox and North were immediately directed to send their seals to the palace by their under secretaries; and Pitt was appointed first lord of the treasury and chancellor of the exchequer.

The general opinion was, that there would be an immediate dissolution.

But Pitt wisely determined to give the public feeling time to gather strength. On this point he differed from his kinsman Temple. The consequence was, that Temple, who had been appointed one of the secretaries of state, resigned his office forty-eight hours after he had accepted it, and thus relieved the new government from a great load of unpopularity; for all men of sense and honor, however strong might be their dislike of the India bill, disapproved of the manner in which that bill had been thrown out. Temple carried away with him the scandal which the best friends of the new government could not but lament. The fame of the young prime minister preserved its whiteness. He could declare with perfect truth that, if unconstitutional machinations had been employed, he had been no party to them.

He was, however, surrounded by

difficulties and dangers. In the House of Lords, indeed, he had a majority; nor could any orator of the opposition in that assembly be considered as a match for Thurlow, who was now again chancellor, or for Camden, who cordially supported the son of his old friend Chatham. But in the other house there was not a single eminent speaker among the official men who sat round Pitt. His most useful assistant was Dundas, who, though he had not eloquence, had sense, knowledge, readiness, and boldness. On the opposite benches was a powerful majority, led by Fox, who was supported by Burke, North, and Sheridan. The heart of the young minister, stout as it was, almost died within him. He could not once close his eyes on the night which followed Temple's resignation. But, whatever his internal emotions might be, his language and deportment indicated nothing but unconquerable firmness and haughty confidence in his own powers. His contest against the House of Commons lasted from the 17th of December, 1783, to the 8th of March, 1784. In sixteen divisions the opposition triumphed. Again and again the King was requested to dismiss his ministers. But he was determined to go to Germany rather than yield. Pitt's resolution never wavered. The cry of the nation in his favor became vehement and almost furious. Addresses assuring him of public support came up daily from every part of the kingdom. The freedom of the city of London was presented to him in a gold box. He went in state to receive this mark of distinction. He was sumptuously feasted in Grocers' Hall; and the shopkeepers of the Strand and Fleet Street illuminated their houses in his honor. These things could not but produce an effect within the walls of parliament. The ranks of the majority began to waver; a few passed over to the enemy; some skulked away; many were for capitulating while it was still possible to capitulate with the honors of war. Negotiations were opened with the view of forming an administration on a wide basis, but they had scarcely been opened when they were closed. The opposition demanded, as a preliminary article of the treaty, that Pitt should resign the treasury; and with this demand Pitt steadfastly refused to comply. While the contest was raging, the clerkship of the Pells, a sinecure place for life, worth three thousand a-year, and tenable with a seat in the House of Commons, became vacant. The appointment was with the chancellor of the exchequer; nobody doubted that he would appoint himself; and nobody could have blamed him if he had done so; for such sinecure offices had always been defended on the ground that they enabled a few men of eminent abilities and small incomes to live without any profession, and to devote themselves to the service of the state. Pitt, in spite of the remonstrances of his friends, gave the Pells to his father's old adherent, Colonel Barré, a man distinguished by talent and eloquence, but poor and afflicted with blindness. By this arrangement a pension which the Rockingham administration had granted to Barré was saved to the public. Never was there a happier stroke of policy. About treaties, wars, expeditions, tariffs, budgets, there will always be room for dispute. The policy which is applauded by half the nation may be condemned by the other half. But pecuniary disinterestedness everybody comprehends. It is a great thing for a man who has only three hundred a-year to be able to show that he considers three thousand a-year as mere dirt beneath his feet, when compared with the public interest and the public esteem. Pitt had his reward. No minister was ever more rancorously libelled; but even when he was known to be overwhelmed with debt, when millions were passing through his hands, when the wealthiest magnates of the realm were soliciting him for marquisates and garters, his bitterest enemies did not dare to accuse him of touching unlawful gain.

At length the hard fought fight ended. A final remonstrance, drawn up by Burke with admirable skill, was carried on the 8th of March by a single vote in a full house. Had the experiment been repeated, the supporters of the coalition would probably have been in a minority. But the supplies had been voted; the mutiny bill had been passed; and the parliament was dissolved.

The popular constituent bodies all over the country were in general enthusiastic on the side of the new government. A hundred and sixty of the supporters of the coalition lost their seats. The first lord of the treasury himself came in at the head of the poll for the university of Cambridge. His young friend, Wilberforce, was elected knight of the great shire of York, in opposition to the whole influence of the Fitzwilliams, Cavendishes, Dundases, and Saviles. In the midst of such triumphs Pitt completed his twenty-fifth year. He was now the greatest subject that England had seen during many generations. He domineered absolutely over the cabinet, and was the favorite at once of the sovereign, of the parliament, and of the nation. His father had never been so powerful, nor Walpole, nor Marlborough.

This narrative has now reached a point, beyond which a full history of the life of Pitt would be a history of England, or rather of the whole civilized world; and for such a history this is not the proper place. Here a very slight sketch must suffice; and in that sketch prominence will be given to such points as may enable a reader who is already acquainted with the general course of events, to form a just notion of the character of the man on whom so much depended.

If we wish to arrive at a correct judgment of Pitt's merits and defects, we must never forget that he belonged to a peculiar class of statesmen, and that he must be tried by a peculiar standard. It is not easy to compare him fairly with such men as Ximenes and Sully, Richelieu and Oxenstiern,

John De Witt and Warren Hastings. The means by which those politicians governed great communities were of quite a different kind from those which Pitt was under the necessity of employing. Some talents, which they never had any opportunity of showing that they possessed, were developed in him to an extraordinary degree. In some qualities, on the other hand, to which they owe a large part of their fame, he was decidedly their inferior. They transacted business in their closets, or at boards where a few confidential councillors sat. It was his lot to be born in an age and in a country in which parliamentary government was completely established; his whole training from infancy was such as fitted him to bear a part in parliamentary government; and from the prime of his manhood to his death, all the powers of his vigorous mind were almost constantly exerted in the work of parliamentary government. He accordingly became the greatest master of the whole art of parliamentary government that has ever existed, a greater than Montague or Walpole, a greater than his father Chatham or his rival Fox, a greater than either of his illustrious successors Canning and Peel.

Parliamentary government, like every other contrivance of man, has its advantages and its disadvantages. On the advantages there is no need to dilate. The history of England during the hundred and seventy years which have elapsed since the House of Commons became the most powerful body in the state, her immense and still growing prosperity, her freedom, her tranquillity, her greatness in arts, in sciences, and in arms, her maritime ascendency, the marvels of her public credit, her American, her African, her

Australian, her Asiatic empires sufficiently prove the excellence of her institutions. But those institutions, though excellent, are assuredly not perfect. Parliamentary government is government by speaking. In such a government, the power of speaking is the most highly prized of all the qualities which a politician can possess; and that power may exist, in the highest degree, without judgment, without fortitude, without skill in reading the characters of men or the signs of the times, without any knowledge of the principles of legislation or of political economy, and without any skill in diplomacy or in the administration of war. Nay, it may well happen that those very intellectual qualities which give a peculiar charm to the speeches of a public man, may be incompatible with the qualities which would fit him to meet a pressing emergency with promptitude and firmness. It was thus with Charles Townshend. It was thus with Windham. It was a privilege to listen to those accomplished and ingenious orators. But in a perilous crisis they would have been found far inferior in all the qualities of rulers to such a man as Oliver Cromwell, who talked nonsense, or as William the Silent, who did not talk at all. When parliamentary government is established, a Charles Townshend or a Windham will almost always exercise much greater influence than such men as the great Protector of England, or as the founder of the Batavian commonwealth. In such a government, parliamentary talent, though quite distinct from the talents of a good executive or judicial officer, will be a chief qualification for executive and judicial office. From the Book of Dignities a curious list might be made out of chancellors ignorant of the principles of equity, and first lords of the admiralty ignorant of the principles of navigation, of colonial ministers who could not repeat the names of the colonies, of lords of the treasury who did not know the difference between funded and unfunded debt, and of secretaries of the India board who did not know whether the Mahrattas were Mahometans or Hindoos. On these grounds, some persons, incapable of seeing more than one side of a question, have pronounced parliamentary government a positive evil, and have maintained that the administration would be greatly improved if the power, now exercised by a large assembly, were transferred to a single person. Men of sense will probably think the remedy very much worse than the disease, and will be of opinion that there would be small gain in exchanging Charles Townshend and

Windham for the prince of the peace, or the poor slave and dog Steenie.

Pitt was emphatically the man of parliamentary government, the type of his class, the minion, the child, the spoiled child, of the House of Commons. For the House of Commons he had a hereditary, an infantine love. Through his whole boyhood, the House of Commons was never out of his thoughts, or out of the thoughts of his instructors. Reciting at his father's knee, reading Thucydides and Cicero into English, analyzing the great Attic speeches on the Embassy and on the Crown, he was constantly in training for the conflicts of the House of Commons. He was a distinguished member of the House of Commons at twenty-one. The ability which he had displayed in the House of Commons made him the most powerful subject in Europe before he was twenty-five. It would have been happy for himself and for his country if his elevation had been deferred. Eight or ten years, during which he would have had leisure and opportunity for reading and reflection, for foreign travel, for social intercourse and free exchange of thought on equal terms with a great variety of companions, would have supplied what, without any fault on his part, was wanting to his powerful intellect. He had all the knowledge that he could be expected to have; that is to say, all the knowledge that a man can acquire while he is a student at Cambridge, and all the knowledge that a man can acquire when he is first lord of the treasury and chancellor of the exchequer. But the stock of general information which he brought from college, extraordinary for a boy, was far inferior to what Fox possessed, and beggarly when compared with the massy, the splendid, the various treasures laid up in the large mind of Burke. After Pitt became minister, he had no leisure to learn more than was necessary for the purposes of the day which was passing over him. What was necessary for those purposes such a man could learn with little difficulty. He was surrounded by experienced and able public servants. He could at any moment command their best assistance. From the stores which they produced his vigorous mind rapidly collected the materials for a good parliamentary case: and that was enough. Legislation and administration were with him secondary matters. To the work of framing statutes, of negotiating treaties, of organizing fleets and armies, of sending forth expeditions, he gave only the leavings of his time and the dregs of his fine intellect. The strength and sap of his mind were all drawn in a different direction. It was when the House of Commons was to be convinced and persuaded that he put forth all his powers.

Of those powers we must form our estimate chiefly from tradition; for of all the eminent speakers of the last age, Pitt has suffered most from the reporters. Even while he was still living, critics remarked that his eloquence could not be preserved, that he must be heard to be appreciated. They more than once applied to him the sentence in which Tacitus describes the fate of a senator whose rhetoric was admired in the Augustan age: "Haterii canorum illud et profluens cum ipso simul exstinctum est." There is, however, abundant evidence that nature had bestowed on Pitt the talents of a great orator; and those talents had been developed in a very peculiar manner; first by his education, and secondly by the high official position to which he rose early, and in which he passed the greater part of his public life.

At his first appearance in parliament he showed himself superior to all his contemporaries in command of language. He could pour forth a long succession of round and stately periods, without premeditation, without ever pausing for a word, without ever repeating a word, in a voice of silver clearness, and with a pronunciation so articulate that not a letter was slurred over. He had less amplitude of mind and less richness of imagination than Burke, less ingenuity than Windham, less wit than Sheridan, less perfect mastery of dialectical fence, and less of that highest sort of eloquence which consists of reason and passion fused together, than Fox. Yet the almost unanimous judgment of those who were in the habit of listening to that remarkable race of men placed Pitt, as a speaker, above Burke, above Windham, above Sheridan, and not below Fox. His declamation was copious, polished, and splendid. In power of sarcasm he was probably not surpassed by any speaker, ancient or modern; and of this formidable weapon he made merciless use. In two parts of the oratorical art which are of the highest value to a minister of state he was singularly expert. No man knew better how to be luminous or how to be obscure. When he wished to be understood he never failed to make himself understood. He could with ease present to his audience, not perhaps an exact or profound, but a clear, popular, and plausible view of the most extensive and complicated subject. Nothing was out of place; nothing was forgotten; minute details, dates, sums of money, were all faithfully preserved in his memory. Even intricate questions of finance, when explained by him, seemed clear to the plainest man among his hearers. On the other hand, when he did not wish to be explicit—and no man who is at the head of affairs always wishes to be explicit—he had a marvellous power of saying nothing in language which left on his audience the impression that he had said a great deal. He was at once the only man who could open a budget without notes, and the only man who, as Windham said, could speak that most elaborately evasive and unmeaning of human compositions, a King's speech, without premeditation.

The effect of oratory will always, to a great extent, depend on the character of the orator. There perhaps never were two speakers whose eloquence had more of what may be called the race, more of the flavor imparted by moral qualities, than Fox and Pitt. The speeches of Fox owe a great part of their charm to that warmth and softness of heart, that sympathy with human suffering, that admiration for every thing great and beautiful, and that hatred of cruelty and injustice, which interest and delight us even in the most defective reports. No person, on the other hand, could hear Pitt without perceiving him to be a man of high, intrepid, and commanding spirit, proudly conscious of his own rectitude and of his own intellectual superiority, incapable of the low vices of fear and envy, but too prone to feel and to show disdain. Pride, indeed, pervaded the whole man, was written in the harsh, rigid lines of his face, was marked by the way in which he walked, in which he sat, in which he stood, and, above all, in which he bowed. Such pride, of course, inflicted many wounds. It may confidently be affirmed that there cannot be found, in all the ten thousand invectives written against Fox, a word indicating that his demeanor had ever made a single personal enemy. On the other hand, several men of note who had been partial to Pitt, and who to the last continued to approve his public conduct and to support his administration, Cumberland, for example, Boswell, and Matthias, were so much irritated by the contempt with which he treated them, that they complained in print of their wrongs. But his pride, though it made him bitterly disliked by individuals, inspired the great body of his followers in parliament and throughout the country with respect and confidence. They took him at his own valuation. They saw that his self-esteem was not that of an upstart, who was drunk with good luck and with applause, and who, if fortune turned, would sink from arrogance into abject humility. It was that of the magnanimous man so finely described by Aristotle in the Ethics, of the man who thinks himself worthy of great things, being in truth worthy. It sprang from a consciousness of great powers and great virtues, and was never so conspicuously displayed as in the midst of difficulties and dangers which would have unnerved and bowed down any ordinary mind. It was closely connected, too, with an ambition which had no mixture of low cupidity. There was something noble in the cynical disdain with which the mighty minister scattered riches and titles to right and left among those who valued them, while he spurned them out of his own way. Poor himself, he was surrounded by friends on whom he had bestowed three thousand, six thousand, ten thousand a-year. Plain Mister himself, he had made more lords than any three ministers that had preceded him. The garter, for which the first dukes in the kingdom were contending, was repeatedly offered to him, and offered in vain.

The correctness of his private life added much to the dignity of his public character. In the relations of son, brother, uncle, master, friend, his conduct was exemplary. In the small circle of his intimate associations, he was amiable, affectionate, even playful. They loved him sincerely; they regretted him long; and they would hardly admit that he who was so kind and gentle with them, could be stern and haughty with others. He indulged, indeed, somewhat too freely in wine, which he had early been directed to take as a medicine, and which use had made a necessary of life to him. But it was very seldom that any indication of undue excess could be detected in his tones or gestures; and, in truth, two bottles of port were little more to him than two dishes of tea. He had, when he was first introduced into the clubs of Saint James's Street, shown a strong taste for play; but he had the prudence and the resolution to stop before this taste had acquired the strength of habit. From the passion which generally exercises the most tyrannical dominion over the young he possessed an immunity, which is probably to be ascribed partly to his temperament, and partly to his situation. His constitution was feeble: he was very shy; and he was very busy. The strictness of his morals furnished such buffoons as Peter Pindar and Captain Morris with an inexhaustible theme for merriment of no very delicate kind. But the great body of the middle class of Englishmen could not see the joke.

They warmly praised the young statesman for commanding his passions, and for covering his frailties, if he had frailties, with decorous obscurity, and would have been very far indeed from thinking better of him if he had vindicated himself from the taunts of his enemies by taking under his protection a Nancy Parsons or a Marianne Clark.

No part of the immense popularity which Pitt long enjoyed is to be attributed to the eulogies of wits and poets. It might have been naturally expected that a man of genius, of learning, of taste, an orator whose diction was often compared to that of Tully, the representative, too, of a great university, would have taken a peculiar pleasure in befriending eminent writers, to whatever political party they might have belonged. The love of literature had induced Augustus to heap benefits on Pompeians, Somers to be the protector of nonjurors, Harley to make the fortunes of Whigs. But it could not move Pitt to show any favor even to Pittites. He was doubtless right in thinking that, in general, poetry, history, and philosophy ought to be suffered, like calico and cutlery, to find their proper price in the market, and that to teach men of letters to look habitually to the state for their recompense, is bad for the state and bad for letters. Assuredly nothing can be more absurd or mischievous than to waste the public money in bounties, for the purpose of inducing people who ought to be weighing out grocery or measuring out drapery, to write bad or middling books. But, though the sound rule is that authors should be left to be remunerated by their readers, there will, in every generation, be a few exceptions to this rule. To distinguish these special cases from the masses, is an employment well worthy of the faculties of a great and accomplished ruler; and Pitt would assuredly have had little difficulty in finding such cases. While he was in power, the greatest philologist of the age, his own contemporary at Cambridge, was reduced to earn a livelihood by the lowest literary drudgery, and to spend in writing squibs for the Morning Chronicle years to which we might have owed an all but perfect text of the whole tragic and comic drama of Athens. The greatest historian of the age, forced by poverty to leave his country, completed his immortal work on the shores of Lake Leman. The political heterodoxy of Porson, and the religious heterodoxy of Gibbon, may perhaps be pleaded in defence of the minister by whom those eminent men were neglected. But there were other cases in which no such excuse could be set up. Scarcely had

Pitt obtained possession of unbounded power, when an aged writer of the highest eminence, who had made very little by his writings, and who was sinking into the grave under a load of infirmities and sorrows, wanted five or six hundred pounds to enable him, during the winter or two which might still remain to him, to draw his breath more easily in the soft climate of Italy. Not a farthing was to be obtained; and before Christmas the author of the English Dictionary and of the lives of the poets, had gasped his last in the river fog and coal smoke of Fleet Street. A few months after the death of Johnson appeared the Task, incomparably the best poem that any Englishman then living had produced—a poem, too, which could hardly fail to excite in a well-constituted mind, a feeling of esteem and compassion for the poet, a man of genius and virtue, whose means were scanty, and whom the most cruel of all the calamities incident to humanity had made incapable of supporting himself by vigorous and sustained exertion. Nowhere had Chatham been praised with more enthusiasm, or in verse more worthy of the subject, than in the Task. The son of Chatham, however, contented himself with reading and admiring the book, and left the author to starve. The pension which, long after, enabled poor Cowper to close his melancholy life, unmolested by duns and bailiffs, was obtained for him by the strenuous kindness of Lord Spencer. What a contrast between the way in which Pitt acted towards Johnson, and the way in which Lord Grey acted towards his political enemy Scott, when Scott, worn out by misfortune and disease, was advised to try the effect of the Italian air! What a contrast between the way in which

Pitt acted towards Cowper, and the way in which Burke, a poor man and out of place, acted towards Crabbe! Even Dundas, who made no pretensions to literary taste, and was content to be considered as a hard-headed and somewhat coarse man of business, was, when compared with his eloquent and classically educated friend, a Mæcenas or a Leo. Dundas made Burns an exciseman, with seventy pounds a year; and this was more than Pitt, during his long tenure of power, did for the encouragement of letters. Even those who may think that it is, in general, no part of the duty of a government to reward literary merit, will hardly deny that a government, which has much lucrative church preferment in its gift, is bound, in distributing that preferment, not to overlook divines whose writings have rendered great service to the cause of religion. But it seems never to have occurred to Pitt that he lay under any such obligation. All the theological works of the numerous bishops whom he made and translated are not, when put together, worth fifty pages of the Horæ Paulinæ, of the Natural Theology, or of the Views of the Evidences of Christianity. But on Paley the all-powerful minister never bestowed the smallest benefice. Artists Pitt treated as contemptuously as writers. For painting he did simply nothing. Sculptors, who had been selected to execute monuments voted by parliament, had to haunt the ante-chambers of the treasury during many years before they could obtain a farthing from him. One of them, after vainly soliciting the minister for payment during fourteen years, had the courage to present a memorial to the King, and thus obtained tardy and ungracious justice. Architects it was absolutely necessary to employ; and the worst that could be found seemed to have been employed. Not a single fine public building of any kind or in any style was erected during his long administration. It may be confidently affirmed that no ruler whose abilities and attainments would bear any comparison with his has ever shown such cold disdain for what is excellent in arts and letters.

His first administration lasted seventeen years. That long period is divided by a strongly marked line into two almost exactly equal parts. The first part ended and the second began in the autumn of 1792. Throughout both parts Pitt displayed in the highest degree the talents of a parliamentary leader. During the first part he was a fortunate, and, in many respects, a skilful administrator. With the difficulties which he had to encounter during the second part he was altogether incapable of contending: but his eloquence and his perfect mastery of the tactics of the House of Commons concealed his incapacity from the multitude.

The eight years which followed the general election of 1784 were as tranquil and prosperous as any eight years in the whole history of England. Neighboring nations which had lately been in arms against her, and which had flattered themselves that, in losing her American colonies, she had lost a chief source of her wealth and of her power, saw, with wonder and vexation, that she was more wealthy and more powerful than ever. Her trade increased. Her manufactures flourished. Her exchequer was full to overflowing. Very idle apprehensions were generally entertained that the public debt, though much less than a third of the debt which we now bear with ease, would be found too heavy for the strength of the nation. Those apprehensions might not perhaps have been easily quieted by reason. But Pitt quieted them by a juggle. He succeeded in persuading first himself, and then the whole nation, his opponents included, that a new sinking fund, which, so far as it differed from former sinking funds, differed for the worst, would, by virtue of some mysterious power of propagation belonging to money, put into the pocket of the public creditor great sums not taken out of the pocket of the tax-payer. The country, terrified by a danger which was no danger, hailed with delight and boundless confidence a remedy which was no remedy. The minister was almost universally extolled as the greatest of financiers. Meanwhile both the branches of the House of Bourbon found that England was as formidable an antagonist as she had ever been. France had formed a plan for reducing Holland to vassalage. But England interposed, and France receded. Spain interrupted by violence the trade of our merchants with the regions near the Oregon. But England armed, and Spain receded. Within the island there was profound tranquillity. The King was, for the first time, popular. During the twenty-three years which had followed his accession he had not been loved by his subjects. His domestic virtues were acknowledged. But it was generally thought that the good qualities by which he was distinguished in private life were wanting to his political character. As a sovereign, he was resentful, unforgiving, stubborn, cunning. Under his rule the country had sustained cruel disgraces and disasters; and every one of those disgraces and disasters was imputed to his strong antipathies, and to his perverse obstinacy in the wrong. One statesman after another complained that he had been induced by royal caresses, entreaties, and promises, to undertake the direction of affairs at a difficult conjuncture, and that, as soon as he had, not without sullying his fame and alienating his best friends, served the turn for which he was wanted, his ungrateful master began to intrigue against him, and to canvass against him. Grenville, Rockingham, Chatham, men of widely different characters, but all three upright and high-spirited, agreed in thinking that the Prince under whom they had successively held the highest place in the government, was one of the most insincere of mankind. His confidence was reposed, they said, not in those known and responsible counsellors to whom he had delivered the seals of office, but in secret advisers who stole up the back stairs into his closet. In parliament, his ministers, while defending themselves against the attacks of the opposition in front, were perpetually, at his instigation, assailed on the flank or in the rear by a vile band of mercenaries who called themselves his friends. These men constantly, while in possession of lucrative places in his service, spoke and voted against bills which he had authorized the first lord of the treasury or the secretary of state to bring in. But from the day in which Pitt was placed at the head of affairs there was an end of secret influence. His haughty and aspiring spirit was not to be satisfied with the mere show of power. Any attempt to undermine him at court, any mutinous movement among his followers in the House of Commons, was certain to be at once put down. He had only to tender his resignation; and he could dictate his own terms. For he, and he alone, stood between the King and the coalition. He was therefore little less than mayor of the palace. The nation loudly applauded the King for having the wisdom to repose entire confidence in so excellent a minister. His Majesty's private virtues now began to produce their full effect. He was generally regarded as the model of a respectable country gentleman, honest, good-natured, sober, religious. He rose early: he dined temperately: he was strictly faithful to his wife: he never missed church: and at church he never missed a response. His people heartily prayed that he might long reign over them; and they prayed the more heartily, because his virtues were set off to the best advantage by the vices and follies of the Prince of Wales, who lived in close intimacy with the chiefs of the opposition.

How strong this feeling was in the public mind, appeared signally on one great occasion. In the autumn of 1788 the King became insane. The opposition, eager for office, committed the great indiscretion of asserting that the heir apparent had, by the fundamental laws of England, a right to be Regent with the full powers of royalty. Pitt, on the other hand, maintained it to be the constitutional doctrine that, when a sovereign is, by reason of infancy, disease, or absence, incapable of exercising the regal functions, it belongs to the estates of the realm to determine who shall be the vicegerent, and with what portion of the executive authority such vicegerent shall be intrusted. A long and violent contest followed, in which Pitt was supported by the great body of the people with as much enthusiasm as during the first months of his administration. Tories with one voice applauded him for defending the sick-bed of a virtuous and unhappy sovereign against a disloyal faction and an undutiful son. Not a few Whigs applauded him for asserting the authority of parliaments and the principles of the revolution, in opposition to a doctrine which seemed to have too much affinity with the servile theory of indefeasible hereditary right. The middle class, always zealous on the side of decency and the domestic virtues, looked forward with dismay to a reign resembling that of Charles II. The palace, which had now been, during thirty years, the pattern of an English home, would be a public nuisance, a school of profligacy. To the good King's repast of mutton and lemonade, despatched at three o'clock, would succeed midnight banquets, from which the guests would be carried home speechless. To the backgammon board at which the good King played for a little silver with his equerries, would succeed faro tables, from which young patricians who had sat down rich would rise up beggars. The drawing-room, from which the frown of the Queen had repelled a whole generation of frail beauties, would now be again what it had been in the days of Barbara Palmer and Louisa de Querouaile. Nay, severely as the public reprobated the Prince's many illicit attachments, his one virtuous attachment was reprobated more severely still. Even in grave and pious circles his Protestant mistresses gave less scandal than his Popish wife. That he must be Regent nobody ventured to deny. But he and his friends were so unpopular that Pitt could, with general approbation, propose to limit the powers of the Regent by restrictions to which it would have been impossible to subject a prince beloved and trusted by the country. Some interested men, fully expecting a change of administration, went over to the opposition. But the majority, purified by these desertions, closed its ranks, and presented a more firm array than ever to the enemy. In every division Pitt was victorious. When at length, after a stormy interregnum of three months, it was announced, on the very eve of the inauguration of the Regent, that the King was himself again, the nation was wild with delight. On the evening of the day on which his Majesty resumed his functions, a spontaneous illumination, the most general that had ever been seen in England, brightened the whole vast space from Highgate to Tooting, and from Hammersmith to Greenwich. On the day on which he returned thanks in the cathedral of his capital, all the horses and carriages within a hundred miles of London were too few for the multitudes which flocked to see him pass through the streets. A second illumination followed, which was even superior to the first in magnificence. Pitt with difficulty escaped from the tumultuous kindness of an innumerable multitude, which insisted on drawing his coach from St. Paul's churchyard to Downing Street. This was the moment at which his fame and fortune may be said to have reached the zenith. His influence in the closet was as great as that of Carr or Villiers had been. His dominion over the parliament was more absolute than that of Walpole or Pelham had been. He was at the same time as high in the favor of the populace as ever Wilkes or Sacheverell had been. Nothing did more to raise his character than his noble poverty. It was well known that, if he had been dismissed from office after more than five years of boundless power, he would hardly have carried out with him a sum sufficient to furnish the set of chambers in which, he cheerfully declared, he meant to resume the practice of the law. His admirers, however, were by no means disposed to suffer him to depend on daily toil for his daily bread. The voluntary contributions which were awaiting his acceptance in the city of London alone would have sufficed to make him a rich man. But it may be doubted whether his haughty spirit would have stooped to accept a provision so honorably earned and so honorably bestowed.

To such a height of power and glory had this extraordinary man risen at twenty-nine years of age. And now the tide was on the turn. Only ten days after the triumphant procession to St.Paul's, the States-General of France, after an interval of a hundred and seventy-four years, met at Versailles.

The nature of the great Revolution

which followed was long very imperfectly understood in this country. Burke saw much further than any of his contemporaries; but whatever his sagacity descried was refracted and discolored by his passions and his imagination. More than three years elapsed before the principles of the English administration underwent any material change. Nothing could as yet be milder or more strictly constitutional than the minister's domestic policy. Not a single act indicating an arbitrary temper or a jealousy of the people could be imputed to him. He had never applied to parliament for any extraordinary powers. He had never used with harshness the ordinary powers intrusted by the constitution to the executive government. Not a single state prosecution which would even now be called oppressive had been instituted by him. Indeed, the only oppressive state prosecution instituted during the first eight years of his administration was that of Stockdale, which is to be attributed, not to the government, but to the chiefs of the opposition. In office, Pitt had redeemed the pledges which he had, at his entrance into public life, given to the supporters of parliamentary reform. He had, in 1785, brought forward a judicious plan for the improvement of the representative system, and had prevailed on the King, not only to refrain from talking against that plan, but to recommend it to the houses in a speech from the throne.[1] This attempt failed: but there can be little doubt that, if the French Revolution had not produced a violent reaction of public feeling, Pitt would have performed, with

[1] The speech with which the King opened the session of 1785 concluded with an assurance, that His Majesty would heartily concur in every measure which could tend to secure the true principles of the constitution. These words were at the time understood to refer to Pitt's Reform Bill.

little difficulty and no danger, that great work which, at a later period, Lord Grey could accomplish only by means which for a time loosened the very foundations of the commonwealth. When the atrocities of the slave trade were first brought under the consideration of parliament, no abolitionist was more zealous than Pitt. When sickness prevented Wilberforce from appearing in public, his place was most efficiently supplied by his friend the minister. A humane bill, which mitigated the horrors of the middle passage, was, in 1788, carried by the eloquence and determined spirit of Pitt, in spite of the opposition of some of his own colleagues; and it ought always to be remembered to his honor that, in order to carry that bill, he kept the houses sitting, in spite of many murmurs, long after the business of the government had been done, and the appropriation act passed. In 1791 he cordially concurred with Fox in maintaining the sound constitutional doctrine, that an impeachment is not terminated by a dissolution. In the course of the same year the two great rivals contended side by side in a far more important cause. They are fairly entitled to divide the high honor of having added to our statute-book the inestimable law which places the liberty of the press under the protection of juries. On one occasion, and one alone, Pitt, during the first half of his long administration, acted in a manner unworthy of an enlightened Whig. In the debate on the test act, he stooped to gratify the master whom he served, the university which he represented, and the great body of clergymen and country gentlemen on whose support he rested, by talking, with little heartiness, indeed, and with no asperity, the language of a

Tory. With this single exception, his conduct from the end of 1783 to the middle of 1792 was that of an honest friend of civil and religious liberty.

Nor did any thing, during that period, indicate that he loved war, or harbored any malevolent feeling against any neighboring nation. Those French writers who have represented him as a Hannibal sworn in childhood by his father to bear eternal hatred to France, as having, by mysterious intrigues and lavish bribes, instigated the leading Jacobins to commit those excesses which dishonored the Revolution, as having been the real author of the first coalition, know nothing of his character or of his history. So far was he from being a deadly enemy to France, that his laudable attempts to bring about a closer connection with that country by means of a wise and liberal treaty of commerce, brought on him the severe censure of the opposition. He was told in the House of Commons that he was a degenerate son, and that his partiality for the hereditary foes of our island was enough to make his great father's bones stir under the pavement of the Abbey.

And this man, whose name, if he had been so fortunate as to die in 1792, would now have been associated with peace, with freedom, with philanthropy, with temperate reform, with mild and constitutional administration, lived to associate his name with arbitrary government, with harsh laws harshly executed, with alien bills, with gagging bills, with suspensions of the habeas corpus act, with cruel punishments inflicted on some political agitators, with unjustifiable prosecutions instituted against others, and with the most costly and most sanguinary wars of modern times. He lived to be held up to obloquy as the stern oppressor of England, and the indefatigable disturber of Europe. Poets, contrasting his earlier with his later years, likened him sometimes to the apostle who kissed in order to betray, and sometimes to the evil angels who kept not their first estate. A satirist of great genius introduced the fiends of Famine, Slaughter, and Fire, proclaiming that they had received their commission from One whose name was formed of four letters, and promising to give their employer ample proofs of gratitude. Famine would gnaw the multitude till they should rise up against him in madness. The demon of Slaughter would impel them to tear him from limb to limb. But Fire boasted that she alone could reward him as he deserved, and that she would cling round him to all eternity. By the French press and the French tribune every crime that disgraced and every calamity that afflicted France was ascribed to the monster Pitt and his guineas. While the Jacobins were dominant, it was he who had corrupted the Gironde, who had raised Lyons and Bordeaux against the convention, who had suborned Paris to assassinate Lepelletier, and Cecilia Regnault to assasinate Robespierre. When the Thermidorian reaction came, all the atrocities of the Reign of Terror were imputed to him. Collot D'Herbois and Fouquier Thinville had been his pensioners. It was he who had hired the murderers of September, who had dictated the pamphlets of Marat and the Carmagnoles of Barrere, who had paid Lebon to deluge Arras with blood, and Carrier to choke the Loire with corpses.

The truth is, that he liked neither war nor arbitrary government. He was a lover of peace and freedom, driven, by a stress against which it was hardly possible for any will or any intellect to struggle, out of the course to which his inclinations pointed, and for which his abilities and acquirements fitted him, and forced into a policy repugnant to his feelings and unsuited to his talents.

The charge of apostasy is grossly unjust. A man ought no more to be called an apostate because his opinions alter with the opinions of the great body of his contemporaries, than he ought to be called an oriental traveller because he is always going round from west to east with the globe and every thing that is upon it. Between the spring of 1789 and the close of 1792, the public mind of England underwent a great change. If the change of Pitt's sentiments attracted peculiar notice, it was not because he changed more than his neighbors; for in fact he changed less than most of them; but because his position was far more conspicuous than theirs, because he was, till Bonaparte appeared, the individual who filled the greatest space in the eyes of the inhabitants of the civilized world. During a short time the nation, and Pitt, as one of the nation, looked with interest and approbation on the French Revolution. But soon vast confiscations, the violent sweeping away of ancient institutions, the domination of clubs, the barbarities of mobs maddened by famine and hatred, produced a reaction here. The court, the nobility, the gentry, the clergy, the manufacturers, the merchants; in short, nineteen-twentieths of those who had good roofs over their heads and good coats on their backs, became eager and intolerant Antijacobins. This feeling was at least as strong among the minister's adversaries as among his supporters. Fox in vain attempted to restrain his followers. All his genius, all his vast personal influence, could not prevent them from rising up against him in general mutiny. Burke set the example of revolt; and Burke was in no long time joined by Portland, Spencer, Fitzwilliam, Loughborough, Carlisle, Malmesbury, Windham, Elliot. In the House of Commons, the followers of the great Whig statesman and orator diminished from about a hundred and sixty to fifty. In the House of Lords he had but ten or twelve adherents left. There can be no doubt that there would have been a similar mutiny on the ministerial benches, if Pitt had obstinately resisted the general wish. Pressed at once by his master and by his colleagues, by old friends, and by old opponents, he abandoned, slowly and reluctantly, the policy which was dear to his heart. He labored hard to avert the European war. When the European war broke out, he still flattered himself that it would not be necessary for this country to take either side. In the spring of 1792, he congratulated parliament on the prospect of long and profound peace, and proved his sincerity by proposing large remissions of taxation. Down to the end of that year he continued to cherish the hope that England might be able to preserve neutrality. But the passions which raged on both sides of the Channel were not to be restrained. The republicans who ruled France were inflamed by a fanaticism resembling that of the Mussulmans, who, with the Koran in one hand and the sword in the other, went forth, conquering and converting, eastward to the Bay of Bengal, and westward to the Pillars of Hercules. The higher and middle classes of England were animated by a zeal not less fiery than that of the Crusaders who raised the cry of *Deus vult* at Clermont. The impulse which drove the two nations to a collision was not to be arrested by the abilities or by the authority of any single man. As Pitt was in front of his fellows, and towered high above them, he seemed to lead them. But in fact he was violently pushed on by them, and, had he held back but a little more than he did, would have been thrust out of their way or trampled under their feet.

He yielded to the current: and from that day his misfortunes began. The truth is, that there were only two consistent courses before him. Since he did not choose to oppose himself, side by side with Fox, to the public feeling, he should have taken the advice of Burke, and should have availed himself of that feeling to the full extent. If it was impossible to preserve peace, he should have adopted the only policy which could lead to victory. He should have proclaimed a Holy War for religion, morality, property, order, public law, and should have thus opposed to the Jacobins an energy equal to their own. Unhappily he tried to find a middle path; and he found one which united all that was worst in both extremes. He went to war: but he would not understand the peculiar character of that war. He was obstinately blind to the plain fact, that he was contending against a state which was also a sect; and that the new quarrel between England and France, was of quite a different kind from the old quarrels about colonies in America and fortresses in the Netherlands. He had to combat frantic enthusiasm, boundless ambition, restless activity, the wildest and most audacious spirit of innovation; and he acted as if he had to deal with the harlots and fops of the old court at Versailles, with Madame de Pompadour and the Abbé de Bernis. It was pitiable to hear him, year after year, proving to an admiring audience that the wicked republic was exhausted, that she could not hold out, that her credit was gone, that her assignats were not worth more than the paper of which they were made; as if credit was necessary to a government of which the principle was rapine, as if Alboin could not turn Italy into a desert till he had negotiated a loan at five per cent., as if the exchequer bills of Attila had been at par. It was impossible that a man who so completely mistook the nature of a contest could carry on that contest successfully. Great as Pitt's abilities were, his military administration was that of a driveller. He was at the head of a nation engaged in a struggle for life and death, of a nation eminently distinguished by all the physical and all the moral qualities which make excellent soldiers. The resources at his command were unlimited. The parliament was even more ready to grant him men and money than he was to ask for them. In such an emergency, and with such means, such a statesman as Richelieu, as Louvois, as Chatham, as Wellesley, would have created in a few months one of the finest armies in the world, and would soon have discovered and brought forward generals worthy to command such an army. Germany might have been saved by another Blenheim; Flanders recovered by another Ramilies; another Poitiers might have delivered the Royalist and Catholic provinces of France from a yoke which they abhorred, and might have spread terror even to the barriers of Paris. But the fact is, that, after eight years of war, after a vast destruction of life, after an expenditure of wealth far exceeding the expenditure of the American war, of the Seven Years' War, of the war of the Austrian Succession, and of the war of the Spanish Succession united, the English army, under Pitt, was the laughing-stock of all Europe. It could not boast of one single brilliant exploit. It had never shown itself on the continent but to be beaten, chased, forced to re-embark, or forced to capitulate. To take some sugar island in the West Indies, to scatter some mob of half naked Irish peasants, such were the most splendid victories won by the British troops under Pitt's auspices.

The English navy no mismanagement could ruin. But during a long period whatever mismanagement could do was done. The Earl of Chatham, without a single qualification for high pnblic trust, was made, by fraternal partiality, first lord of the admiralty, and was kept in that great post during two years of a war in which the very existence of the state depended on the efficiency of the fleet. He continued to doze away and trifle away the time which ought to have been devoted to the public service, till the whole mercantile body, though generally disposed to support the government, complained bitterly that our flag gave no protection to our trade. Fortunately he was succeeded by George Earl Spencer, one of those chiefs of the Whig party who, in the great schism caused by the French Revolution, had followed Burke. Lord Spencer, though inferior to many of his colleagues as an orator, was decidedly the best administrator among them. To him it was owing that a long and gloomy succession of days of fasting, and, most emphatically, of humiliation, was interrupted, twice in the short space of eleven months, by days of thanksgiving for great victories.

It may seem paradoxical to say that the incapacity which Pitt showed in all that related to the conduct of the war is, in some sense, the most decisive proof that he was a man of very extraordinary abilities. Yet this is the simple truth. For assuredly one-tenth part of his errors and disasters would have been fatal to the power and influence of any minister who had not possessed, in the highest degree, the talents of a parliamentary leader. While his schemes were confounded, while his predictions were falsified, while the coalitions which he had labored to form were falling to pieces, while the expeditions which he had sent forth at enormous cost were ending in rout and disgrace, while the enemy against whom he was feebly contending was subjugating Flanders and Brabant, the electorate of Mentz and the electorate of Treves, Holland, Piedmont, Liguria, Lombardy, his authority over the House of Commons was constantly becoming more and more absolute. There was his empire. There were his victories, his Lodi and his Arcola, his Rivoli and his Marengo. If some great misfortune, a pitched battle lost by the allies, the annexation of a new department to the French republic, a sanguinary insurrection in Ireland, a mutiny in the fleet, a panic in the city, a run on the bank, had spread dismay through the ranks of his majority, that dismay lasted only till he rose from the treasury bench, drew up his haughty head, stretched his arm with commanding gesture, and poured forth, in deep and sonorous tones, the lofty language of inextinguishable hope and inflexible resolution. Thus, through a long and calamitous period, every disaster that happened without the walls of parliament was regularly followed by a triumph within them. At length he had no longer an opposition to encounter. Of the great party which had contended against him during the first eight years of his administration, more than one half now marched under his standard, with his old competitor the Duke of Portland at their head; and the rest had, after many vain struggles, quitted the field in despair. Fox had retired to the shades of St. Anne's Hill, and had there found, in the society of friends whom no vicissitude could estrange from him, of a woman whom he tenderly loved, and of the illustrious dead of Athens, of Rome, and of Florence, ample compensation for all the misfortunes of his public life. Session followed session with scarcely a single division. In the eventful year 1799, the largest minority that could be mustered against the government was twenty-five.

In Pitt's domestic policy there was at this time assuredly no want of vigor. While he offered to French Jacobinism a resistance so feeble that it only encouraged the evil which he wished to suppress, he put down English Jacobinism with a strong hand. The habeas corpus act was repeatedly suspended. Public meetings were placed under severe restraints. The government obtained from parliament power to send out of the country aliens who were suspected of evil designs; and that power was not suffered to be idle. Writers who propounded doctrines adverse to monarchy and aristocracy, were proscribed and punished without mercy. It was hardly safe for a republican to avow his political creed over his beefsteak and his bottle of port at a chophouse. The old laws of Scotland against sedition, laws which were considered by Englishmen as barbarous, and which a succession of governments had suffered to rust, were now furbished up and sharpened anew. Men of cultivated minds and polished manners were, for offences which at Westminster would have been treated as mere misdemeanors, sent to herd with felons at Botany Bay. Some reformers, whose opinions were extravagant, and whose language was intemperate, but who had never dreamed of subverting the government by physical force, were indicted for high treason, and were saved from the gallows only by the righteous verdicts of juries. This severity was at the time loudly applauded by alarmists whom fear had made cruel, but will be seen in a very different light by posterity. The truth is, that the Englishmen who wished for a revolution were, even in number, not formidable, and, in every thing but number, a faction utterly contemptible, without arms, or funds, or plans, or organization, or leader. There can be no doubt that Pitt, strong as he was in the support of the great body of the nation, might easily have repressed the turbulence of the discontented minority by firmly yet temperately enforcing the ordinary law. Whatever vigor he showed during this unfortunate part of his life, was vigor out of place and season. He was all feebleness and languor in his conflict with the foreign enemy who was really to be dreaded, and reserved all his energy and resolution for the domestic enemy, who might safely have been despised.

One part only of Pitt's conduct during the last eight years of the eighteenth century deserves high praise. He was the first English minister who formed great designs for the benefit of Ireland.

The manner in which the Roman Catholic population of that unfortunate country had been kept down during many generations seemed to him unjust and cruel; and it was scarcely possible for a man of his abilities not to perceive that, in a contest against the Jacobins, the Roman Catholics were his natural allies. Had he been able to do all that he wished, it is probable that a wise and liberal policy would have averted the rebellion of 1798. But the difficulties which he encountered were great, perhaps insurmountable; and the Roman Catholics were, rather by his misfortune than by his fault, thrown into the hands of the Jacobins. There was a third great rising of the Irishry against the Englishry, a rising not less formidable than the risings of 1641 and 1689. The Englishry remained victorious; and it was necessary for Pitt, as it had been necessary for Oliver Cromwell and

William of Orange before him, to consider how the victory should be used. It is only just to his memory to say that he formed a scheme of policy, so grand and so simple, so righteous and so humane, that it would alone entitle him to a high place among statesmen. He determined to make Ireland one kingdom with England, and, at the sme time, to relieve the Roman Catholic laity from civil disabilities, and to grant a public maintenance to the Roman Catholic clergy. Had he been able to carry these noble designs into effect, the Union would have been a Union indeed. It would have been inseparably associated in the minds of the great majority of Irishmen with civil and religious freedom; and the old parliament in College Green would have been regretted only by a small knot of discarded jobbers and oppressors, and would have been remembered by the body of the nation with the loathing and contempt due to the most tyrannical and the most corrupt assembly, that had ever sat in Europe. But Pitt could execute only one half of what he had projected. He succeeded in obtaining the consent of the parliaments of both kingdoms to the Union: but that reconciliation of races and sects, without which the Union could exist only in name, was not accomplished. He was well aware that he was likely to find difficulties in the closet. But he flattered himself that, by cautious and dexterous management, those difficulties might be overcome. Unhappily, there were traitors and sycophants in high place, who did not suffer him to take his own time and his own way, but prematurely disclosed his scheme to the King, and disclosed it in the manner most likely to irritate and alarm a weak and diseased mind.

His Majesty absurdly imagined that his coronation oath bound him to refuse his assent to any bill for relieving Roman Catholics from civil disabilities. To argue with him was impossible. Dundas tried to explain the matter, but was told to keep his Scotch metaphysics to himself. Pitt, and Pitt's ablest colleagues, resigned their offices. It was necessary that the King should make a new arrangement. But by this time his anger and distress had brought back the malady which had, many years before, incapacitated him for the discharge of his functions. He actually assembled his family, read the Coronation oath to them, and told them that, if he broke it, the Crown would immediately pass to the House of Savoy. It was not until after an interregnum of several weeks that he regained the full use of his small faculties, and that a ministry after his own heart was at length formed.

The materials out of which he had to construct a government were neither solid nor splendid. To that party, weak in numbers, but strong in every kind of talent, which was hostile to the domestic and foreign policy of his late advisers, he could not have recourse. For that party, while it differed from his late advisers on every point on which they had been honored with his approbation, cordially agreed with them as to the single matter which had brought on them his displeasure. All that was left to him was to call up the rear rank of the old ministry to form the front rank of a new ministry. In an age pre-eminently fruitful of parliamentary talents, a cabinet was formed containing hardly a single man who, in parliamentary talents, could be considered as even of the second rate. The most important offices in the state were bestowed on decorous and laborious mediocrity. Henry Addington was at the head of the treasury. He had been an early, indeed a hereditary friend of Pitt, and had by Pitt's influence been placed, while still a young man, in the chair of the House of Commons. He was universally admitted to have been the best speaker that had sat in that chair since the retirement of Onslow. But nature had not bestowed on him very vigorous faculties; and the highly respectable situation which he had long occupied with honor, had rather unfitted than fitted him for the discharge of his new duties. His business had been to bear himself evenly between contending factions. He had taken no part in the war of words; and he had always been addressed with marked deference by the great orators who thundered against each other from his right and from his left. It was not strange that when, for the first time, he had to encounter keen and vigorous antagonists, who dealt hard blows without the smallest ceremony, he should have been awkward and unready, or that the air of dignity and authority which he had acquired in his former post, and of which he had not divested himself, should have made his helplessness laughable and pitiable. Nevertheless, during many months, his power seemed to stand firm. He was a favorite with the King, whom he resembled in narrowness of mind, and to whom he was more obsequious than Pitt had ever been. The nation was put into high good humor by a peace with France. The enthusiasm with which the upper and middle classes had rushed into the war had spent itself. Jacobinism was no longer formidable. Everywhere there was a strong reaction against what was called the atheistical and anarchical philosophy of the eighteenth century. Bonaparte, now First Consul, was busy in constructing out of the ruins of old institutions a new ecclesiastical establishment and a new order of knighthood. That nothing less than the dominion of the whole civilized world would satisfy his selfish ambition was not yet suspected; nor did even wise men see any reason to doubt that he might be as safe a neighbor as any prince of the House of Bourbon had been. The treaty of Amiens was therefore hailed by the great body of the English people with extravagant joy. The popularity of the minister was for the moment immense. His want of parliamentary ability was, as yet, of little consequence; for he had scarcely any adversary to encounter. The old opposition, delighted by the peace, regarded him with favor. A new opposition had indeed been formed by some of the late ministers, and was led by Grenville in the House of Lords, and by Windham in the House of Commons. But the new opposition could scarcely muster ten votes, and was regarded with no favor by the country. On Pitt the ministers relied as on their firmest support. He had not, like some of his colleagues, retired in anger. He had expressed the greatest respect for the conscientious scruple which had taken pessession of the royal mind ; and he had promised his successors all the help in his power. In private his advice was at their service. In parliament he took his seat on the bench behind them ; and, in more than one debate, defended them with powers far superior to their own. The King perfectly understood the value of such assistance. On one occasion, at the palace, he took the old minister and the new minister aside. "If we three," he said, "keep together, all will go well."

But it was hardly possible, human nature being what it is, and, more especially, Pitt and Addington being what they were, that this union should be durable. Pitt, conscious of superior powers, imagined that the place which he had quitted was now occupied by a mere puppet which he had set up, which he was to govern while he suffered it to remain, and which he was to fling aside as soon as he wished to resume his old position. Nor was it long before he began to pine for the power which he had relinquished. He had been so early raised to supreme authority in the state, and had enjoyed that authority so long, that it had become necessary to him. In retirement his days passed heavily. He could not, like Fox, forget the pleasures and cares of ambition in the company of Euripides or Herodotus. Pride restrained him from intimating, even to his dearest friends, that he wished to be again minister. But he thought it strange, almost ungrateful, that his wish had not been divined, that it had not been anticipated, by one whom he regarded as his deputy.

Addington, on the other hand, was by no means inclined to descend from his high position. He was, indeed, under a delusion much resembling that of Abon Hassan in the Arabian tale. His brain was turned by his short and unreal caliphate. He took his elevation quite seriously, attributed it to his own merit, and considered himself as one of the great triumvirate of English statesmen, as worthy to make a third with Pitt and Fox.

Such being the feelings of the late minister and of the present minister, a rupture was inevitable; and there was no want of persons bent on making that rupture speedy and violent.

Some of these persons wounded Addington's pride by representing him as a lackey, sent to keep a place on the treasury bench till his master should find it convenient to come. Others took every opportunity of praising him at Pitt's expense. Pitt had waged a long, a bloody, a costly, an unsuccessful war. Addington had made peace. Pitt had suspended the constitutional liberties of Englishmen. Under Addington those liberties were again enjoyed. Pitt had wasted the public resources. Addington was carefully nursing them. It was sometimes but too evident that these compliments were not unpleasing to Addington. Pitt became cold and reserved. During many months he remained at a distance from London. Meanwhile his most intimate friends, in spite of his declarations that he made no complaint, and that he had no wish for office, exerted themselves to effect a change of ministry. His favorite disciple, George Canning, young, ardent, ambitious, with great powers and great virtues, but with a temper too restless and a wit too satirical for his own happiness, was indefatigable. He spoke; he wrote; he intrigued; he tried to induce a large number of the supporters of the government to sign a round robin desiring a change; he made game of Addington and of Addington's relations in a succession of lively pasquinades. The minister's partisans retorted with equal acrimony, if not with equal vivacity. Pitt could keep out of the affray only by keeping out of politics altogether; and this it soon became impossible for him to do. Had Napoleon, content with the first place among the sovereigns of the Continent, and with a military reputation surpassing that of Marlborough or of Turenne, devoted himself to the noble task of making France happy by mild administration and wise legislation, our country might have long continued to tolerate a government of fair intentions and feeble abilities. Unhappily, the treaty of Amiens had scarcely been signed, when the restless ambition and the insupportable insolence of the First Consul convinced the great body of the English people that the peace, so eagerly welcomed, was only a precarious armistice. As it became clearer and clearer that a war for the dignity, the independence, the very existence of the nation was at hand, men looked with increasing uneasiness on the weak and languid cabinet, which would have to contend against an enemy who united more than the power of Lewis the Great to more than the genius of Frederick the Great. It is true that Addington might easily have been a better war minister than Pitt, and could not possibly have been a worse. But Pitt had cast a spell on the public mind. The eloquence, the judgment, the calm and disdainful firmness which he had, during many years, displayed in parliament, deluded the world into the belief that he must be eminently qualified to superintend every department of politics; and they imagined, even after the miserable failures of Dunkirk, of Quiberon, and of the Helder, that he was the only statesman who could cope with Bonaparte. This feeling was nowhere stronger than among Addington's own colleagues. The pressure put on him was so strong, that he could not help yielding to it: yet, even in yielding, he showed how far he was from knowing his own place. His first proposition was, that some insignificant nobleman should be first lord of the treasury and nominal head of the administration, and that the real power should be divided between Pitt and himself, who were to be secretaries of state. Pitt, as might have been expected, refused even to discuss such a scheme, and talked of it with bitter mirth. "Which secretaryship was offered to you?" his friend Wilberforce asked. "Really," said Pitt, "I had not the curiosity to inquire." Addington was frightened into bidding higher. He offered to resign the treasury to Pitt, on condition that there should be no extensive change in the government. But Pitt would listen to no such terms. Then came a dispute such as often arises after negotiations orally conducted, even when the negotiators are men of strict honor. Pitt gave one account of what had passed; Addington gave another; and though the discrepancies were not such as necessarily implied any intentional violation of truth on either side, both were greatly exasperated.

Meanwhile the quarrel with the First Consul had come to a crisis. On the 16th of May 1803, the King sent a message calling on the House of Commons to support him in withstanding the ambitious and encroaching policy of France; and on the 22d, the House took the message into consideration.

Pitt had now been living many months in retirement. There had been a general election since he had spoken in parliament, and there were two hundred members who had never heard him. It was known that on this occasion he would be in his place, and curiosity was wound up to the highest point. Unfortunately, the short-hand writers were, in consequence of some mistake, shut out on that day from the gallery, so that the newspapers contained only a very meagre report of the proceedings. But several accounts of what passed are extant; and of those accounts, the most interesting is contained in an unpublished letter written by a very young member, John William Ward, afterwards Earl of Dudley. When Pitt rose, he was received with loud cheering. At every pause in his speech there was a burst of applause. The peroration is said to have been one of the most animated and magnificent ever heard in parliament. "Pitt's speech," Fox wrote a few days later, "was admired very much, and very justly. I think it was the best he ever made in that style." The debate was adjourned; and on the second night Fox replied in an oration which, as the most zealous Pittites were forced to acknowledge, left the palm of eloquence doubtful. Addington made a pitiable appearance between the two great rivals; and it was observed that Pitt, while exhorting the Commons to stand resolutely by the executive government against France, said not a word indicating esteem or friendship for the prime minister.

War was speedily declared. The First Consul threatened to invade England at the head of the conquerors of Belgium and Italy, and formed a great camp near the Straits of Dover. On the other side of those Straits the whole population of our island was ready to rise up as one man in defence of the soil. At this conjuncture, as at some other great conjunctures in our history, the conjuncture of 1660, for example, and the conjuncture of 1688, there was a general disposition among honest and patriotic men to forget old quarrels, and to regard as a friend every person who was ready, in the existing emergency, to do his part towards the saving of the state. A coalition of all the first men in the country would, at that moment, have been as popular as the coalition of 1783 had been unpopular. Alone in the kingdom the King looked with perfect complacency on a cabinet in which no man superior to himself in genius was to be found, and was so far from being willing to admit all his ablest subjects to office, that he was bent on excluding them all.

A few months passed before the different parties which agreed in regarding the government with dislike and contempt, came to an understanding with each other. But in the spring of 1804, it became evident that the weakest of ministries would have to defend itself against the strongest of oppositions; an opposition made up of three oppositions, each of which would, separately, have been formidable from ability, and which, when united, were also formidable from number. The party which had opposed the peace, headed by Grenville and Windham, and the party which had opposed the renewal of the war, headed by Fox, concurred in thinking that the men now in power were incapable of either making a good peace or waging a vigorous war. Pitt had, in 1802, spoken for peace against the party of Grenville, and had, in 1803, spoken for war against the party of Fox. But of the capacity of the cabinet, and especially of its chief, for the conduct of great affairs, he thought as meanly as either Fox or Grenville. Questions were easily found on which all the enemies of the government could act cordially together. The unfortunate first lord of the treasury, who had, during the earlier months of his administration, been supported by Pitt on one side, and by Fox on the other, now had to answer Pitt, and to be answered by Fox. Two sharp debates, followed by close divisions, made him weary of his post. It was known, too, that the upper house was even more hostile to him than the lower, that the Scotch representative peers wavered, that there were signs of mutiny among the bishops. In the cabinet itself there was discord, and, worse than discord, treachery. It was necessary to give way: the ministry was dissolved; and the task of forming a government was intrusted to Pitt.

Pitt was of opinion that there was now an opportunity, such as had never before offered itself, and such as might never offer itself again, of uniting in the public service, on honorable terms, all the eminent talents of the kingdom. The passions to which the French Revolution had given birth were extinct. The madness of the innovator and the madness of the alarmist had alike had their day. Jacobinism and Anti-jacobinism had gone out of fashion together. The most liberal statesman did not think that season propitious for schemes of parliamentary reform; and the most conservative statesman could not pretend that there was any occasion for gagging bills and suspensions of the habeas corpus act. The great struggle for independence and national honor occupied all minds; and those who were agreed as to the duty of maintaining that struggle with vigor, might well postpone to a more convenient time all disputes about matters comparatively unimportant. Strongly impressed by these considerations, Pitt wished to form a ministry including all the first men in the country. The treasury he reserved for himself; and to Fox he proposed to assign a share of power little inferior to his own.

The plan was excellent; but the King would not hear of it. Dull, obstinate, unforgiving, and, at that time, half mad, he positively refused to admit Fox into his service. Anybody else, even men who had gone as far as Fox, or further than Fox, in what his Majesty considered as Jacobinism, Sheridan, Grey, Erskine, should be graciously received; but Fox never. During several hours Pitt labored in vain to reason down this senseless antipathy. That he was perfectly sincere there can be no doubt; but it was not enough to be sincere; he should have been resolute. Had he declared himself determined not to take office without Fox, the royal obstinacy would have given way, as it gave way, a few months later, when opposed to the immutable resolution of Lord Grenville. In an evil hour Pitt yielded. He flattered himself with the hope that, though he consented to forego the aid of his illustrious rival, there would still remain ample materials for the formation of an efficient ministry. That hope was cruelly disappointed. Fox entreated his friends to leave personal considerations out of the question, and declared that he would support, with the utmost cordiality, an efficient and patriotic ministry from which he should be himself excluded. Not only his friends, however, but Grenville, and Grenville's adherents, answered with one voice, that the question was not personal; that a great constitutional principle was at stake, and that they would not take office while a man eminently qualified to render service to the commonwealth was placed under a ban merely because he was disliked at court. All that was left to Pitt was to construct a government out of the wreck of Addington's feeble administration. The small circle of his personal retainers furnished him with a very few useful assistants, particularly Dundas, who had been created Viscount Melville, Lord Harrowby, and Canning.

Such was the inauspicious manner in which Pitt entered on his second administration. The whole history of that administration was of a piece with the commencement. Almost every month brought some new disaster or disgrace. To the war with France was soon added a war with Spain. The opponents of the minister were numerous, able, and active. His most useful coadjutors he soon lost. Sickness deprived him of the help of Lord Harrowby. It was discovered that Lord Melville had been guilty of highly culpable laxity in transactions relating to public money. He was censured by the House of Commons, driven from office, ejected from the privy council, and impeached of high crimes and misdemeanors. The blow fell heavy on Pitt. It gave him, he said in parliament, a deep pang; and, as he uttered the word pang, his lip quivered; his voice shook; he paused; and his hearers thought that he was about to burst into tears. Such tears shed by Eldon would have moved nothing but laughter. Shed by the warm-hearted and open-hearted Fox, they would have moved sympathy, but would have caused no surprise. But a tear from Pitt would have been something portentous. He suppressed his emotion, however, and proceeded with his usual majestic self-possession.

His difficulties compelled him to resort to various expedients. At one time Addington was persuaded to accept office with a peerage; but he brought no additional strength to the government. Though he went through the form of reconciliation, it was impossible for him to forget the past.

While he remained in place he was jealous and punctilious; and he soon retired again. At another time Pitt renewed his efforts to overcome his master's aversion to Fox; and it was rumored that the King's obstinacy was gradually giving way. But, meanwhile, it was impossible for the minister to conceal from the public eye the decay of his health and the constant anxiety which gnawed at his heart. His sleep was broken. His food ceased to nourish him. All who passed him in the park, all who had interviews with him in Downing Street, saw misery written in his face. The peculiar look which he wore during the last months of his life was often pathetically described by Wilberforce, who used to call it the Austerlitz look.

Still the vigor of Pitt's intellectual faculties, and the intrepid haughtiness of his spirit, remained unaltered. He had staked every thing on a great venture. He had succeeded in forming another mighty coalition against the French ascendency. The united forces of Austria, Russia, and England might, he hoped, oppose an insurmountable barrier to the ambition of the common enemy. But the genius and energy of Napoleon prevailed. While the English troops were preparing to embark for Germany, while the Russian troops were slowly coming up from Poland, he, with rapidity unprecedented in modern war, moved a hundred thousand men from the shores of the Ocean to the Black Forest, and compelled a great Austrian army to surrender at Ulm. To the first faint rumors of this calamity Pitt would give no credit. He was irritated by the alarms of those around him. "Do not believe a word of it," he said: "it is all a fiction." The next day he received a Dutch newspaper containing the capitulation. He knew no Dutch. It was Sunday; and the public offices were shut. He carried the paper to Lord Malmesbury, who had been minister in Holland; and Lord Malmesbury translated it. Pitt tried to bear up, but the shock was too great; and he went away with death in his face.

The news of the battle of Trafalgar arrived four days later, and seemed for a moment to revive him. Forty-eight hours after that most glorious and most mournful of victories had been announced to the country came the Lord Mayor's day; and Pitt dined at Guildhall. His popularity had declined. But on this occasion the multitude, greatly excited by the recent tidings, welcomed him enthusiastically, took off his horses in Cheapside, and drew his carriage up King Street. When his health was drunk, he returned thanks in two or three of those stately sentences of which he had a boundless command. Several of those who heard him laid up his words in their hearts; for they were the last words that he ever uttered in public: "Let us hope that England, having saved herself by her energy, may save Europe by her example."

This was but a momentary rally. Austerlitz soon completed what Ulm had begun. Early in December Pitt had retired to Bath, in the hope that he might there gather strength for the approaching session. While he was languishing there on his sofa arrived the news that a decisive battle had been fought and lost in Moravia, that the coalition was dissolved, that the Continent was at the feet of France. He sank down under the blow. Ten days later, he was so emaciated that his most intimate friends hardly knew him. He came up from Bath by slow journeys, and, on the 11th of January, 1806, reached his villa at Putney. Parliament was to meet on the 21st. On the 20th was to be the parliamentary dinner, at the house of the first lord of the treasury, in Downing Street; and the cards were already issued. But the days of the great minister were numbered. The only chance for his life, and that a very slight chance, was, that he should resign his office, and pass some months in profound repose. His colleagues paid him very short visits, and carefully avoided political conversation. But his spirit, long accustomed to dominion, could not, even in that extremity, relinquish hopes which everybody but himself perceived to be vain. On the day on which he was carried into his bed-room at Putney, the Marquess Wellesley, whom he had long loved, whom he had sent to govern India, and whose administration had been eminently able, energetic, and successful, arrived in London after an absence of eight years. The friends saw each other once more. There was an affectionate meeting, and a last parting. That it was a last parting, Pitt did not seem to be aware. He fancied himself to be recovering, talked on various subjects cheerfully, and with an unclouded mind, and pronounced a warm and discerning eulogium on the Marquess's brother Arthur. "I never," he said, "met with any military man with whom it was so satisfactory to converse." The excitement and exertion of this interview were too much for the sick man. He fainted away; and Lord Wellesley left the house, convinced that the close was fast approaching.

And now members of parliament were fast coming up to London. The chiefs of the opposition met for the purpose of considering the course to be taken on the first day of the session. It was easy to guess what would be the language of the King's speech, and of the address which would be moved in answer to that speech. An amendment condemning the policy of the government had been prepared, and was to have been proposed in the House of Commons by Lord Henry Petty, a young nobleman who had already won for himself that place in the esteem of his country which, after the lapse of more than half a century, he still retains. He was unwilling, however, to come forward as the accuser of one who was incapable of defending himself. Lord Grenville, who had been informed of Pitt's state by Lord Wellesley, and had been deeply affected by it, earnestly recommended forbearance; and Fox, with characteristic generosity and good nature, gave his voice against attacking his now helpless rival. "Sunt lacrymæ rerum," he said, "et mentem mortalia tangunt." On the first day, therefore, there was no debate. It was rumored that evening that Pitt was better. But on the following morning his physicians pronounced that there were no hopes. The commanding faculties of which he had been too proud were begining to fail. His old tutor and friend, the Bishop of Lincoln, informed him of his danger, and gave such religious advice and consolation as a confused and obscured mind could receive. Stories were told of devout sentiments fervently uttered by the dying man. But these stories found no credit with any body who knew him. Wilberforce pronounced it impossible that they could be true; "Pitt," he added, "was a man who said less than he thought on such topics." It was asserted in many after-dinner speeches, Grub Street elegies, and academic prize poems and prize declamations, that the great minister died exclaiming, "Oh, my country!" This is a fable; but it is true that the last words which he uttered, while he knew what he said, were broken exclamations about the alarming state of public affairs. He ceased to breathe on the morning of the 23d of January 1806, the twenty-fifth anniversary of the day in which he first took his seat in parliament. He was in his forty-seventh year, and had been, during near nineteen years, first lord of the treasury, and undisputed chief of the administration. Since parliamentary government was established in England, no English statesman has held supreme power so long. Walpole, it is true, was first lord of the treasury during more than twenty years, but it was not till Walpole had been some time first lord of the treasury that he could be properly called prime minister.

It was moved in the House of Commons that Pitt should be honored with a public funeral, and a monument. The motion was opposed by Fox in a speech which deserves to be studied as a model of good taste and good feeling. The task was the most invidious that ever an orator undertook; but it was performed with a humanity and delicacy which were warmly acknowledged by the mourning friends of him who was gone. The motion was carried by 288 votes to 89.

The 22d of February was fixed for the funeral. The corpse having lain in state during two days in the Painted Chamber, was borne with great pomp to the northern transept of the Abbey. A splendid train of princes, nobles, bishops and privy councillors followed. The grave of Pitt had been made near to the spot where his great father lay, near also to the spot where his great rival was soon to lie. The sadness of the assistants was beyond that of ordinary mourners. For he whom they were committing to the dust, had died of sorrows and anxieties of which none of the survivors could be altogether without a share. Wilberforce, who carried the banner before the hearse, described the awful ceremony with deep feeling. As the coffin descended into the earth, he said, the eagle face of Chatham from above seemed to look down with consternation into the dark house which was receiving all that remained of so much power and glory.

All parties in the House of Commons readily concurred in voting forty thousand pounds to satisfy the demands of Pitt's creditors. Some of his admirers seemed to consider the magnitude of his embarrassments as a circumstance highly honorable to him; but men of sense will probably be of a different opinion. It is far better, no doubt, that a great minister should carry his contempt of money to excess, than that he should contaminate his hands with unlawful gain. But it is neither right nor becoming in a man to whom the public has given an income more than sufficient for his comfort and dignity, to bequeath to that public a great debt, the effect of mere negligence and profusion. As first lord of the treasury and chancellor of the exchequer, Pitt never had less than six thousand a year, besides an excellent house. In 1792 he was forced by his royal master's friendly importunity to accept for life the office of warden of the Cinque Ports, with near four thousand a year more. He had neither wife nor child: he had no needy relations: he had no expensive tastes: he had no long election bills. Had he given but a quarter of an hour a week to the regulation of his household, he would have kept his expenditure within bounds. Or, if he could not spare even a quarter of an hour a week for that purpose, he had numerous friends, excellent men of business, who would have been proud to act as his stewards. One of those friends, the chief of a great commercial house in the city, made an attempt to put the establishment in Downing Street to rights; but in vain. He found that the waste of the servants' hall was almost fabulous. The quantity of butcher's meat charged in the bills was nine hundredweight a week. The consumption of poultry, of fish, of tea, was in proportion. The character of Pitt would have stood higher if, with the disinterestedness of Pericles and of De Witt, he had united their dignified frugality.

The memory of Pitt has been assailed, times innumerable, often justly, often unjustly; but it has suffered much less from his assailants than from his eulogists. For, during many years, his name was the rallying cry of a class of men with whom, at one of those terrible conjunctures which confound all ordinary distinctions, he was accidentally and temporarily connected, but to whom, on almost all great questions of principle, he was diametrically opposed. The haters of parliamentary reform called themselves Pittites, not choosing to remember that Pitt made three motions for parliamentary reform, and that, though he thought that such a reform could not safely be made while the passions excited by the French Revolution were raging, he never uttered a word indicating that he should not be prepared at a more convenient season to bring the question forward a fourth time. The toast of Protestant ascendency was drunk on Pitt's birthday by a set of Pittites, who could not but be aware that Pitt had resigned his office because he could not carry Catholic emancipation. The defenders of the Test Act called themselves Pittites, though they could not be ignorant that Pitt had laid before George the Third unanswerable reasons for abolishing the Test Act. The enemies of free trade called themselves Pittites, though Pitt was far more deeply imbued with the doctrines of Adam Smith than either Fox or Grey. The very negro-drivers invoked the name of Pitt, whose eloquence was never more conspicuously displayed than when he spoke of the wrongs of the negro. This mythical Pitt, who resembles the genuine Pitt as little as the Charlemagne of Ariosto resembles the Charlemagne of Eginhard, has had his day. History will vindicate the real man from calumny disguised under the semblance of adulation, and will exhibit him as what he was, a minister of great talents, honest intentions, and liberal opinions, pre-eminently qualified, intellectually and morally, for the part of a parliamentary leader, and capable of administering with prudence and moderation the government of a prosperous and tranquil country; but unequal to surprising and terrible emergencies, and liable, in such emergencies, to err gievously, both on the side of weakness and on the side of violence.

www.ingramcontent.com/pod-product-compliance
Lightning Source LLC
LaVergne TN
LVHW050530100826
845148LV00002B/500